Hops, Malt, Yeast, and Water

A Novice's Guide to Craft Beer and Homebrewing

Ph.D. STAN KAMINSKI

© Copyright 2024 - All rights reserved.

The content contained within this book may not be reproduced, duplicated, or transmitted without direct written permission from the author or the publisher.

Under no circumstances will any blame or legal responsibility be held against the publisher or author for any damages, reparation, or monetary loss due to the information contained within this book. Either directly or indirectly.

Legal Notice:

This book is copyright-protected. This book is only for personal use. You cannot amend, distribute, sell, use, quote, or paraphrase any part of this book's content without the author's or publisher's consent.

Disclaimer Notice:

Please note the information contained within this document is for educational and entertainment purposes only. All effort has been executed to present accurate, up-to-date, reliable, and complete information. No warranties of any kind are declared or implied. Readers acknowledge that the author does not render legal, financial, medical, or professional advice. The content within this book has been derived from various sources. Please consult a licensed professional before attempting any techniques outlined in this book.

By reading this document, the reader agrees that under no circumstances is the author responsible for any losses, direct or indirect, which are incurred as a result of the use of the information contained within this document, including, but not limited to, — errors, omissions, or inaccuracies.

Table of Content

Hops, Malt, Yeast, and Water

Introduction

Ever since ancient humans first discovered fermented grains, beer has held a celebrated place in civilizations around the world. What began as a humble porridge-like beverage has evolved over millennia into an art form with infinite possibilities for flavor, aroma and character. Today, home brewing lets anyone channel this rich heritage by manifesting their own small-batch beers customized to individual tastes and curiosities.

This comprehensive guide explores the complete process of crafting beer from scratch at home using natural ingredients, basic equipment, and traditional brewing techniques. Through easy-to-follow recipes and in-depth theory, both novice and experienced brewers will gain skills to produce an array of beer styles rivaling commercial offerings. Far beyond the realm of bland lagers, this book unlocks the compelling nuances of ales, stouts, lambics, wheats and everything in between.

We begin by examining beer's remarkable origins dating back over 7,000 years to ancient Mesopotamia where gruel-like porridge dregs spontaneously fermented, delighting early humans. This happy accident sparked the birth of brewing ingenuity across Old World cultures from ancient Egypt to medieval Europe. Tracing beer's evolution sheds light on modern ingredients and processes still employed today.

Subsequent chapters provide a full education in the four core ingredients enabling beer's magic: malted barley providing fermentable sugars, hops lending bitterness and aroma, yeast facilitating fermentation, and water comprising 90% of beer's anatomy.

We explore the diverse roles each element plays while guiding readers through selecting optimal varieties for their desired beer profiles. Careful grain sourcing, hop blending, yeast wrangling and water chemistry all contribute to superior taste.

As the book progresses, focus turns to the full brewing cycle from mashing grains through the boil, fermentation scheduling, clarifying and packaging the finished product. Step-by-step walkthroughs explain essential brewing equipment while illustrating techniques like mashing, lautering, chilling, aerating and racking. With these basics down, artistic exploration begins by formulating tried-and-true recipes across beer's major style categories, encompassing ales, lagers, stouts and more.

Throughout the process, discussions on mitigating common mistakes provide insight on troubleshooting problems that inevitably arise from time to time. With patience and a little chemistry knowledge, brewers can analyze and correct awry batches before they become undrinkable. Issues like off-flavors, poor foam, unwanted aromas and cloudy appearance all signal opportunities for dialing in procedures.

Once brewers gain basic experience and confidence, chapters on advanced methods like temperature-controlled fermentation, adding fruits, spices or other adjuncts offer opportunities for unleashing creativity. Perfecting techniques to develop rich complex flavors, clarity and effervescence polishes beers into masterpieces worthy of judging and competition entry.

Upon mastering the normal brewing regimen, readers receive coaching on periodically deep cleaning their equipment to avoid cross-contamination and unwanted off-flavors from residue buildup.

We also cover beer tasting strategies to hone palates, basic pairings with cheese and food to accentuate each element, and tips on serving home brews including volumes, glassware and temperature.

Beer has captivated humankind for ages because it represents a perfect confluence of art, science and community. Even in today's age of hyper-industrialized corporate brewing, anyone can still tap into that communal joy by developing their own local flavors at home. The immense diversity of beer styles, ingredients and creativity offers a bottomless well for experimentation across lifetimes.

So ready your brew pot and fire, because this guide equips you with the knowledge to turn that basic bread porridge into a masterpiece of fermentation and flavor. Let your journey into home brewing begin and reignite that ancient spark of spontaneity that first illuminated humankind toward beer's delights!

Chapter 1

A Brief History of Beer

Few things have shaped human civilization as much as the discovery of beer. Before we settled into cities, grew crops, or forged empires, our ancestors were brewing. From Mesopotamia to China, people across the ancient world came to the same miraculous realization - that allowing grain and water to ferment could yield a magical elixir capable of nourishing, intoxicating, and bringing communities together.

As we'll explore in this chapter, beer provided the pivotal impetus for the Agricultural Revolution approximately 10,000 years ago. Only once our nomadic ancestors began intentionally cultivating cereal crops for brewing did permanent large-scale agriculture and settlements become possible. Barley and wheat fields served to sate the thirst for beer, a staple drink and sacred centerpiece across most ancient cultures.

The Sumerians of ancient Mesopotamia revered beer as a gift from the gods and even recorded hymns praising it, like the 4,000-year-old Hymn to Ninkasi. Ancient Chinese tribes brewed a beer-like substance called kui some 9,000 years ago. Ancient Greeks and Romans fermented cereal grains into primitive beers. Wherever agriculture sprouted, beer's bubbly goodness flowed soon after.

From pharaohs to peasants, beer was the beverage of choice across ancient societies. It reigned for thousands of years as humanity's drink of choice until the past few centuries. Safe, nutritious, and pleasurable, beer unlocked new possibilities for coming together in the community and fueled the growth of civilization itself.

Gods Nectar: How Beer Drove the Agricultural Revolution

Given beers' universal popularity across ancient cultures, one might reasonably ask - which group invented this beloved beverage? But perhaps more astonishingly, compelling evidence suggests that beer existed long before any established 'civilizations' did.

Our hunter-gatherer ancestors had stumbled upon fermented fruit juices and honey wines naturally occurring in the wild. But actual beer as we know it - made from cereal grains - seems to have arisen concurrently across multiple cultures as tribes transitioned from nomadic lifestyles to agricultural living between 12,000-10,000 years ago.

Rather than pinpointing a single ancient people who 'invented' beer, it emerged organically across cultures from Mesopotamia to China as a tasty byproduct of settling down and cultivating cereal crops. These nutrient-rich grasses, like barley, were first grown not for bread or porridge but for brewing beer.

Early agriculturalists soon unlocked the magic of malting - allowing sprouted grain to release sugars, then brewing a sweet wort to ferment with yeast into beer. Almost as quickly as our ancestors began actively growing cereal crops, they discovered how to turn grains into gold-nourishing, inebriating beer.

This alcoholic nectar of the gods held such importance across nascent civilizations that some anthropologists have credited beer as incentivizing and supporting the pivotal switch from nomadic hunter-gathering to organized agriculture.

Settling down in one fertile place to grow bountiful rows of barley or wheat would have held little appeal without a compelling reason driving this monumental shift. But being able to brew large quantities of delicious beer has been reason enough for our ancestors. Fields of grain meant unlimited beer.

Once agriculture had taken root, cities, trade networks, and entire empires were built upon the foundational shifts enabled by beer. The cereal crops that gave rise to ancient brewing traditions led to food surplus and specialization of labor outside of subsistence food production. Beer lubricated early economies and became a ubiquitous dietary staple and social glue.

From Poison to Societal Bedrock
Given beer's exalted status across nearly all ancient societies as an invaluable nourishment source, social lubricant, and sacred

substance, one might imagine it was universally loved from the outset. But compelling historical evidence suggests beer had much humbler beginnings before ascending to societal superstardom.

Humans' initial reactions upon tasting beer's curious bubbliness were likely similar to most primal encounters with fermentation - suspicion, confusion, and even disgust. Before mastering the science of brewing and fermentation, our ancestors invariably dealt with failed brews that tasted foul or poisoned drinkers.

Early beers were likely inconsistently soured, contaminated with bacteria, utterly flat, or alarmingly cloudy compared to the clear brews we enjoy today. Unappealing aromas and flavors ranging from rotten eggs to burning sensations accompanied humanity's first sips of beer.

Additionally, the mood-altering properties of beer's alcohol content would have been incredibly disorienting to people unaccustomed to chemical intoxication. Our ancestors did not instantly fall in love with those first bizarre and perhaps unpleasant batches of fermented grain broth.

So how did beer progress from toxic muck to become arguably humanity's most culturally important beverage? We have those repulsed yet brave souls daring to sample batches of sour beer repeatedly to thank.

Progress came gradually as brewers learned to preferentially cultivate certain grains, master malting techniques, improve sanitation practices, and isolate beneficial yeast strains from the air. Advances spread unevenly across scattered early civilizations, causing beer quality to remain wildly inconsistent for thousands of years.

Nevertheless, the irresistible draw of beer's enjoyable effects, once perfected, ensured that all ancient cultures with access to cereal grains kept trying to brew this magical substance despite copious failed attempts.

The grains were so highly prized as brewing fodder that they supplanted all other crops as the top agricultural priority. Our determined ancestors recognized that flawless beer might lie just around the corner after enough experimentation. The reward would justify any temporary poisonings.

When Barley Met Yeast: Brewing Perfected

Ancient peoples probably recognized that allowing certain wild grasses to get wet and then set aside created bubbly concoctions leading to euphoria long before they could explain the biological process behind fermentation. Early accidental beers formed a cornerstone upon which agrarian civilization would be erected over thousands of years.

The earliest evidence of actual beer production using malted cereal grains traces back over 12,000 years to the Natufian culture thriving in parts of the Middle East. The Natufians focused their grain agriculture efforts on brewing beer rather than baking bread.

Archaeological excavations suggest they may have enjoyed a primitive form of beer made from a combination of wheat and barley. Remains show the Natufians were actively malting grains, likely to extract fermentable sugars. They also crafted vessels ideal for brewing and drinking beer communally.

Several thousand years after the first proto-beers emerged in the Middle East, East Asian cultures also pivoted hard towards serious beer brewing between 7,000-9,000 years ago. Archaeologists have uncovered underground millet beer brewing production facilities dating back to that period at the Jiahu village site in Henan province, China.

Sophisticated breweries containing specialized pits for steaming the millet, fermentation vessels, drinking cups, and odd strainers confirm deliberate beer making on a large scale was already occurring in Neolithic China. Remarkably advanced for an early agrarian outpost, Jiahu brewed with millet and other grains, honey, grapes, and hawthorn fruit as adjuncts.

From there, practically every civilization with cereal grains quickly developed unique beer traditions. Mesopotamians, Egyptians, Nubians, Chinese, Inca, Maya, Africans. By the time written records emerged, beer was firmly entrenched as the beverage of choice across ancient cultures.

These scattered groups all came to the same realization - allowing grain broths to sit undisturbed invited magic. Wild yeast settled onto the sweet mixture, multiplied and fermented sugars into alcohol and carbon dioxide for uniquely refreshing and intoxicating effects.

Early beer wasn't identical to modern brews, often incorporating unusual grains or adjuncts, lacking hops entirely, and consumed via straws from large vessels instead of individual servings. Nevertheless, those first primitive beers set humanity on a course that would irrevocably shape diet, health, socializing, and economics for thousands of years right up to the present.

Hymns and Hallucinations: Beer as Ceremonial Centerpiece

Once ancient peoples unlocked the secrets to brewing, they rapidly promoted beer from a mere nutritional staple to an exalted centerpiece anchoring religious and community life. Secure access to plentiful amounts of decent - albeit inconsistent - beer allowed early tribal groups and eventual great civilizations to flourish as never before possible.

Yet beyond its critical role in nourishing citizens with vitamins, minerals, carbohydrates, and hydration, beer-filled spiritual and communal voids. The manufacturing process brimmed with ceremony and mystique. Master brewers often donned priestly robes while conjuring each batch of holy drink.

Once ready, beer was central in facilitating public gatherings and private religious communion across many ancient cultures. Imbibing this divine drink forged connections with savored ancestors, gods, or one's soul. Transcendent inspiration frequently arose.

Early societies actively worshipped beer, among other fermented staples like wine or mead, as a heavenly gift directly from its resident gods, enabling all subsequent human progress. Naturally, these cultures made beer a fixture of elaborate tribute ceremonies and feasts aimed at pleasing or communicating with their godly pantheons.

This sacred aura surrounding beer lives on in contemporary times through trappings like the term brewmasters donning monk robes or names like Abbey Ales. But in the ancient world, beer wasn't merely branded using religious motifs for marketing appeal. Brewing and drinking rituals carried the weight of genuine spiritual communion and magical possibility.

While ancient Egyptians buried beer alongside other essential provisions for enjoying the afterlife, the Sumerians wrote adoring hymns to the mystical powers of beer. Poets praised this divine drink, which "makes the heart full of joy and the mind full of cheer." Beer halls doubled as temples where flowing alcohol stoked spiritual transformation above mundane realities.

The Sumerians plighted their troth with beer. As part of binding legal agreements or royal land grants, access to daily rations of grain and bread was guaranteed in writing by the Mes Sec ordinance. But even more crucially, a standard allotment of 5 liters of government-produced beer (known as a sila3) was provided for each citizen daily.

Sumerian beer was consumed through reed straws from large shared vessels, as the drink was generally too thick to guzzle from cups casually. Citizens sucked up this sweet and viscous brew made strong at 8% alcohol from a daily ration large enough to keep spirits soaring morning, noon, and night.

With access to such generous helpings of divine drink secured as a sacred covenant between leaders and citizens, communities prospered in the cradle of civilization. Beer fueled humanity from infancy into culturally thriving adolescence after 200,000 years of nomadic hunting and gathering.

Liquid Loaf: Nutrition from Beer Saves the Day

While beer offered plenty of social, ceremonial, and recreational incentives beckoning our early ancestors towards agriculture and community living, nutrition was the most pragmatic reason it became ubiquitous. Beer provided nourishment and vitamins otherwise scarce when equivalent crop yields were baked into bread alone.

Grain and water constituted up to 80% of the average person's diet across ancient civilizations. Porridge, flatbread, or doughy loaves built from barley, wheat, millet, or corn provided ample carbohydrates but little else nutritionally. Plant and animal protein sources remained inconsistent for most.

Making dough into beer exponentially amplified its nutritional value, however. Fermenting the carbohydrate-rich wort created B Vitamins that were absent in plain dough. Beer also provides plentiful minerals like silicon, nickel, selenium, titanium, and potassium.

Additionally, the alcohol conversion process broke down gluten, making beer's nutrition far more accessible to absorb than dense grain loaves. Children readily drank this liquid bread, thinned from chunky gruel into pleasantly drinkable form. Elders lacking appetite or teeth turned to beer's nutrition when eating solid foods became implausible.

Indeed, beer proved so helpful in nourishing the most vulnerable groups like children, the elderly, or the impoverished that it served as a fundamental welfare system across ancient cities. Standard ration entitlements aimed to keep all citizens functioning happily fed and watered with ample barley beer.

As a liquid food source, beer provided up to half the daily calories in many ancient societies. Egyptian texts analyzed by archaeologists suggest that worker rations and pyramid-building budgets were based on supplying regular beer dispersals to keep operations running smoothly.

Standard daily allotments provided about 3 liters of beer, offering nearly 1,000 calories - plenty to sustain energy levels under a scorching sun even when overall nutrition lagged behind modern standards. Beer served to fill hunger, aid digestion, and wash down otherwise bland fare.

Partially, this reliance on beer instead of water for hydration came from the ubiquity of unsanitary waterways rife with dangerous bacteria, parasites, and waterborne illnesses in urbanizing regions. Whether due to pollution from early mining or fertilizers, lack of sanitation infrastructure as cities boomed, or contamination en route from remote water sources - drinking straight from rivers often proved lethal.

Boiling water and then diluting after it cooled garnered mixed results safety-wise. But fermenting beverages created lethal organic acids even to resilient food-borne pathogens. This antimicrobial quality lasted through storage cycles.

So citizens learned not to sporadically sip room temperature questionable water throughout the day but instead to regularly partake of a comparatively safe daily alcoholic beer accompanied by bread servings. Life expectancy benefitted greatly.

Beyond survival, beer made daily drudgery more bearable and lent comfort when extra provisions ran low. Reliable access to beer provided enough confidence in the food supply to enable couples to bear more offspring. This kept successor lines intact and armies staffed.

When grain stores occasionally ran low, panic and societal unrest soon followed at the threat of sobriety or outright starvation if scarcity continued. But beer had become so beloved and utterly essential that spirits remained merry even under challenging years thanks to the priestly rations.

This scenario has played out across early societies. Beer became the raft carrying humanity through flood or famine. Its well-established role in religious rituals also led to belief in beer's supernatural protective powers against disease or hardship. Cultures fervently prayed to patron gods for salvation and gave thanks by pouring out copious libations of beer.

As the backbone nourishment source beer provided slowly improved over centuries across cultures, it also birthed coveted arts, trade networks, technological innovation, and centralized economies necessary for civilizations to blossom.

Brewers Figured it Out: Inventions Spurred by Beer.

Beer proved so beloved across early societies that improving brewing equipment became a high-priority technological mission akin to modern Space Race ambitions. Refining the processes and tools surrounding beer drove innovation, benefiting unrelated spheres of daily life.

The earliest evidence of beer brewing operations indicates manufacturing happened on a domestic or small group scale but organized enough to require dedicated production areas. Containing the messy brewing procedures safely indoors while producing sizeable volumes for storage and distribution purposes encouraged architectural planning breakthroughs.

Spaces hosting these crucial beer-making steps needed protection from the elements but accommodation for heating or cooling infrastructure depending on climate. Buildings also required sufficient ventilation to limit smoke inhalation from the malting and boil steps, allow steam release, and prevent mold from establishing itself within damp interiors.

Additionally, structures housing beer production faced much heavier sanitation demands than private homes or communal halls. The growth of undesirable microbes and wild yeast strains (or the entry of tiny insects eager to gorge on rich resources inside) could easily ruin entire batches of beer.

So building materials, spatial layouts, heating mechanisms, drainage and waste disposal systems, and cleaning procedures underwent intensive enhancements for early beer factories compared to other buildings that safely stored grain or hosted social gatherings. Breweries birthed cutting-edge construction insights.

But arguably even more influential on technological progress were the container upgrades essential for beer storage and distribution. Moving reliable volumes of fresh beer beyond where it was brewed using vessels made from clay or—later—glass pushed the development of standardized pottery and bottling breakthroughs.

Amphoras, casks, jugs, and eventually bottles grew increasingly sophisticated to meet beer transport challenges as thirst expanded into new communities. Stoppers and seals preventing precious liquid loss or contamination dramatically improved. Egyptians invented a fast pipe and spigot dispensing method. Mesopotamians sculpted triple-layered filtration straws for improved beer freshness even miles from the brewery.

Methods for labeling vessels clearly according to contents using images, symbols, or text also arose due to beer distribution throughout neighborhoods and beyond. Accounting records, tracking allotments, and calculating supplies gave rise to written language and mathematical principles. Right down to the ceremonial drinking tubes appearing in art and records, beer proved a muse for advancement.

If poured into modern glassware, ancient beers would astonish our senses as radically different brews than we class as beer today. Nevertheless, those odd ancestral ales made from grapes or bananas, flavored with tree resins or smoked grains, gently bubbled by wild yeasts, and unsophisticated fermentation laid the structural foundation for all beers to come.

As we now understand it, proper beer arose from a messy evolutionary journey across scattered tribes that each unlocked the cereal grain fermentation puzzle around the same era to birth some of the earliest purpose-driven agriculture.

This beloved beverage the Sumerians called "the best, the most wonderful food of the lands" motivated and nourished the first communities. Beer consumption rituals and production methods birthed gods and art, while technology breakthroughs granting increased volumes birthed trade routes and wealth big enough to erect history's first cities.

Humanity owes much to those first primitive beers, however unrefined or inconsistent they may have tasted. Our love of beer's captivating flavors and mood-elevating effects ensured we kept trying to perfect this magical craft until agriculture, economics, medicine, and entire societies pivoted into existence around it. We have beer to thank for the modern world.

Of course, once agriculture was established nearly everywhere thanks to beer, barley and wheat's delicious fermentable sugars became the obvious choice for brewing across most cultures. Wheat provided balanced flavors with a clean finish, while barley offered versatility for innovation. These foundational brewing grains remain anchored at the heart of most beers today.

While barley's versatility made it the go-to grain for most cultures, unique beer traditions still emerged across scattered early civilizations thanks to factors like locally available cereal crops or wild edible plants, individual water chemistry profiles, ambient yeast strains, innovative brewing vessels, ceremony styles influencing flavor profiles, and storage considerations dictating strength. These diverse brewing approaches using the best regionally available ingredients gave rise to what we now classify as distinct historical beer styles still brewed today.

As agricultural communities stabilized enough for small-scale craft specialization like full-time brewing to arise as a trade option, tiny breweries popped up, churning out their unique take on beer. Local palates grew accustomed to these signature flavors produced from local crops, yeasts, or water. Over generations, indigenous ingredients imparting distinctive sensory qualities grew prized as markers of regional pride.

Ancient brewers actively safeguarded their unique beer recipes as proprietary trade secrets. Unique combinations of fermentable sugars, herbs, spices, fruit, or even tree resins were added during brewing to create signature flavors not easily replicated elsewhere. These customized flavor profiles and production techniques distinguishing one village's ales from the next eventually codified into labeled beer styles during the Middle Ages when hops entered the scene.

Hops, Malt, Yeast, and Water

While beer had enjoyed a long, uncontested reign as the tipple of choice across ancient societies, it looked and tasted radically different in various regions based on grains or adjuncts used, extras tossed in the boil, ambient microflora, water chemistry, vessels, and storage considerations. These diverse ancestral brews set the stage for developing the major beer styles that are still popular today.

Mesopotamian and Egyptian beers were exceptionally thick, sweet, and high-calorie brews, clocking in at around 8-10% alcohol. Brewing intensifies the natural sugars in raw date, pomegranate, fig juice, or else derived extra sugars as starch converted during the malting phase. The resulting syrupy and even slightly chunky consistency was well suited for drinking via long straws.
Ancient brewers added contrasting bitterness by crumbling myrrh, oak galls, ginger, or pungent cyperus herb to balance aggressive sweetness levels from all the residual sugars. Some Egyptian beers gained crisp effervescence by blending with fresh grape or apple cider before fermenting. Others featured energetic bubbles from secondary fermentation in sealed vessels.

Skipping ahead to another famous beer-loving civilization embracing fermentation under hot climates, ancient Teotihuacanos living just north of modern Mexico City concocted their unique style sourced from local crops beginning around 100-750 CE.

Called "pulque," this fizzy milky brew relied not on barley malt for fermentable sugars but instead tapped sweet aguamiel sap straight from the towering maguey cactus dotting the arid landscape. Skilled pulque makers sliced flowering stems to release magic sap, which naturally fermented into a sour, fruity beer bearing hallmarks like tartness, funk, and wild bubbles that still captivate fans today.

Transitioning from hot southern zones to the chilly Gaelic north, rustic beers constructed mainly from bere barley circulated Scotland and Ireland for millennia. This simple yet satisfying grain imparted signature earthy, mildly floral notes defining Irish stouts when malted over slow-burning peat fires.

Grains weren't the only crop-inspiring local beer specialties, however. Grapes are grown for wine and sometimes repurposed into drinks like Portuguese cerveja de most, blending fresh sweet grape juice with malt wort for fermentation into an ancient summer quaffer. Belgian Guezes and Flanders Reds also take cues from grapes. Wheat's clean flavors naturally lend to bubblier summer beers. The indigenous Americas tangled with unusual vegetation like corn for chicha or psychedelic herbs for ritual drinking.

Wild and wacky homebrews prevailed in outposts yet untouched by the stricter Germanic brewing purity laws still centuries away. This unrestricted creativity in local beer recipes and profiles meant no two beers tasted alike from region to region or village. Exotic ales emerged from the boundaries of imagination to fit specialized ceremonial roles or sate unusual fruit-forward preferences.

The resulting spirited diversity in early brewing meant ancient peoples enjoyed access to dozens of unique fermented beverages, all falling under the broad umbrella term of beer but sporting radically different production processes and sensory experiences compared to neighboring groups.

This scenario would remain the status quo for millennia until a fateful Old World leaf migration enabled the stabilization and codification of the major beer styles recognized today.
That leaf delivering a flavor revelation and process overhaul was, of course - hops.

Bitter Herb Unites Beer Styles

While early beer held such sacred status that tweaking traditional local recipes often bordered on blasphemy, bittering herbs and fermented fruit juices still found their way into various grain-based brews as signature regional additions. Hops have grown wild throughout Europe and Asia for millennia. But hops for brewing only gained widespread traction once technology advancements during the early Middle Ages allowed large-scale cultivation and broader distribution of those punchy dried cones into any brew house wishing to improve their beer's flavor and longevity.

The first documented evidence of hop utilization as a deliberate beer bittering agent and preservative emerged around 820 CE within monastery breweries of Northern France and only trickled far beyond regional borders once commercial hop farming operations scaled up by 1000 CE. Within a few centuries, this intriguing herb would migrate throughout continental Europe, forever altering the course of brewing.

When introduced to traditional gruit-style ales ready for disruption, hops' bitter, herbaceous edge and ability to balance sweetness while restricting certain beer spoilage microbes provided a revelation. Brewers had relied upon messy blends of herbs like bog myrtle, yarrow, juniper berries, heather, or other spices for bitterness or masking off beer flavors until that point - with mixed but often mediocre success. Unlike these older gruit components, sustainably harvested dried hops offered remarkable flavor consistency and spoiled far less readily.

Practically, medieval brewers only needed to take one whiff comparing their current beer-bittering blend whole versus the startlingly hopped ales emerging from Cistercian monasteries to recognize game-changing improvement potential. Within a few centuries, such rapid enthusiastic adoption of hops occurred for all major beer styles that the Reinheitsgebot purity law established in 1516 CE in Bavaria, Germany, restricted allowable beer ingredients exclusively to barley, hops, and water (later amended to permit wheat and select yeast once microbiology advanced).

This widespread shift towards dominated hop-based bitterness and increased quality control in manufacturing brewing equipment ushered in the earliest relics of stylistic standards we recognize for beer today by organizing varied base beer sub-styles around a united bittering agent.

Popular wisdom warns against fixing things that aren't broken. Yet tired old rustic gruit-style beers blended from culinary herbs and fermented fruit juices seemed broken once hops came knocking with objectively tastier bittering potential minus the hassle of hodgepodge components.

By the late 1700s, with both bittering and conservation techniques improvements well cemented, brewers enjoyed enough foundational consistency across regions in base grains, bitterness, and fermentation methods to carefully craft dozens of distinct, inherently delicious, and stable enough beer styles still favored today - buoyed by specialty local tweaks when desired but united in production approach thanks to hops.

Novel brews branching beyond traditional boundaries occasionally captivated local fancy across Bavaria, England, and Belgium pockets before fading into obscurity when phenomenally fickle drinkers moved on to the next curiosity. Most of these odd resurrected ancient ales relied upon experimental grains or forgotten herbs instead of hops. Their fleeting resurrection proved less about winning fans back from hopped competition and more about honoring arcane local lore lost long ago.

Compared to ancient counterparts, many modern beer styles likely seem tame or outright boring at first sip. Missing are the chunks of millet or flavor crescendos of resinous spruce tips. Gone is the funky magic of spontaneously fermented cactus sap in terracotta pots. Banished are the aromatic smoky notes from peated malt dried over burning seaweed harvested after autumn storms.

But beer equaled only the total of its ingredients for too long. Brewer's hands were tied trying to elevate beer quality and artistry with one arm's length constrained by local crop inconsistency; you harvested what grew that year. The other arm battled microbes eager to spoil batches and eliminate nuance. Attempts towards better beer seemed doomed by a lack of communication with fellow innovators just one town over. They were also puzzling away at perfecting their craft in isolation using regional crops that grew each harvest.

Hops deliverance fused once fragmented brewers into an interwoven community collectively working towards shared goals of deliciousness and drinkability and celebrating regional agriculture through localized interpretations of now stabilized beer styles classified by overall production methods and ingredient combinations.

They are liberating brewers from the shackles of unpredictability, making room for sophisticated enhancements building upon sound foundations. No longer must brewing improvements arise accidentally or remain insulated as just happy village accidents. Brewing became an intentional artistic practice rather than a customized regional survival necessity alone.

This powerful blending of intention and chaos underpins modern beer's vibrant, boundless identity today. While ancient beer traditions and experimental brews will always retain a revered place, securing callbacks to specialty ingredients upholding cultural heritage, it was only through adopting reliable base bittering that ale evolved from rustic village necessity to a global art form celebrated today in thousands of unique interpretations across 100 distinct style categories - yet traceable back to just four irreplaceable ingredients at its core.

Beer's epic evolutionary arc mirrors - and enables - humanity's improbable path from nomadic hunting and gathering into eventual networked megacities filled with art, ideas, commerce, and community, all fueled by agriculture's bountiful nourishment.

Barley and wheat fields supporting entire early societies would not have reliably taken root if not for the irresistible call of beer. This beloved beverage, parching thirst while forging social connections and powering innovations, remains humanity's longest-running and most influential biochemical technology, improving diet, health, and happiness to this day.

We owe those first tentative brewers puzzling over bubbling buckets of odd-smelling gruel an immense debt of gratitude. Thanks to their maverick palates daring to sample each failed batch, steeling themselves against bitter, ugly early ales or even serious poisoning risks from contaminated drinks, beer was steadily shepherded from a toxic novelty into a beloved essential pillar of civilization itself.

Prost! Let's raise a pint in tribute to beer's magnificent backstory. As we'll explore next, magical barley played an equally formidable part in ascending beer's place in our hearts and history. This versatile cereal grain still anchors the majority of beers today as it has for at least nine thousand years, thanks to unique mashing talents...

Chapter 2

Malted Barley and the Magic of Mashing

Brewers have relied on the alchemical process of malting barley for thousands of years to unlock the sweet treasure hidden within each kernel: fermentable sugars that will fuel the yeast and lead to glorious beer. This chapter explores malted barley—the backbone of beer—and the magic of mashing to extract its goodness. We'll begin by understanding how barley is cultivated, chosen, and coaxed to sprout through malting before it ever reaches the brewery.

Selecting Barley for Malting

As with any craft, quality ingredients lead to quality results. For barley destined to become beer, growers select plump grains with moderate protein levels from varieties that perform well in local growing conditions. High protein can lead to trouble during lagering and filtration, while thin, shriveled barley kernels lack sufficient starch stores to convert to fermentable sugars. The best malting barley varieties balance plumpness and starch content with moderate protein levels below 12 percent. Popular varieties include Maris Otter (England), Copeland and Metcalfe (Canada), and AC Metcalfe or Tradition (USA).

Whether two-row or six-row, all barley begins as seeds that growers carefully sow in spring or fall. As slender green shoots poke through the soil, the young barley plant directs its energy into the seed head forming atop the stalk. Over a few months of growth, sunlight and soil nutrients transform into starch packed tightly into the developing barley kernel. Too little rain stresses the plant, while heavy rains promote rapid growth that washes away starch reserves. Skillful farmers balance these influences through irrigation schedules and harvest their barley crops not by the calendar but by indicators of full maturity.

At harvest, specialized equipment gently reaps ripe barley while minimizing any damage to the grain. Skilled handlers then screen the harvest for optimal starch content and plumpness, rejecting any under-developed, diseased, or damaged grains unfit for malting. This selection process sets aside barley's highest quality offering for transformation into malt—the first step on its journey to the brew kettle and barrel.

Reawakening Barley Through Malting

Transport trucks filled with raw barley depart the fields bound for commercial malting houses. Here, the alchemical malting process will ready the grain for brewing through controlled germination followed by kilning.

Upon delivery, maltsters thoroughly analyze the barley for adequate protein, moisture, and starch levels before accepting the batch. Barley scoring below quality thresholds gets diverted to animal feed and ethanol plants, while subpar batches still edible to humans become "adjunct grains" for supplementing malt in beers. Only premium barley cuts single malt batches.

The best malting barley then undergoes cleaning, grading, and sorting to prepare a consistent batch for steeping. Gentle washing removes debris from the fields, while grading by kernel size brings uniformity. Maltsters tune these steps to match the barley variety's needs before transferring it to steep tanks.

In this first phase of malting, immersion in water triggers enzymatic changes within the dormant seed. As moisture permeates the protective husk and penetrates the starch stores, biological activity resumes within the embryo after months of dormancy. Over two to three days, maltsters closely control steeping temperatures and cycles to encourage the seed to sprout. Too quickly, enzymes develop unevenly; too slowly, the batch risks spoilage.

When the rootlet emerges, signaling the surge of enzymes, the wet barley gets transferred to germination beds. Carefully tended, turned, and tested these next five days allow young shoots and enzymes to develop. By the sixth day, the process reaches a crescendo with enzyme levels peaking: amylases for cleaving starch into sugars and proteases for breaking down hordein proteins. Before the burst of biological activity exhausts the starch supplies, the maltster arrests this newborn plantlet's growth through kilning.

Drying and Curing Malt in the Kiln

Water-laden malt fresh from germination beds contains around 45 percent moisture content. Before it can travel to brew kettles, kilning reduces this moisture level to only 4 percent of the malt's total weight. Temperature and duration of kilning also impart color and flavor characteristics that significantly impact the beer.

To avoid shocking the delicate malt, kilns gently warm incoming green malt beds to as high as 105°F before raising temperatures. Ramping slowly in stages across 20 to 48 hours ensures moisture evaporates steadily. For pale malts, maltsters arrest kilning below 162°F once the desired moisture content drops to around 4 percent.

Higher kilning temperatures intensify flavors and darken the malt from rich gold to chocolate brown.

The crisp dried malt gets cleaned, sorted, and analyzed for quality consistency with moisture content stabilized. Select batches will blend with other malts to balance flavor profiles for different brewers' needs. Excess rootlets break away easily from the dried grain before sizing and polishing to prepare the malt for delivery to breweries. Packaged in breathable sacks, properly kilned malt boasts a shelf life of up to 24 months. Thanks to this extended freshness, maltsters can build inventories that provide brewers flexibility in recipes and harvest variability.

From this point forward, brewers use time-honored techniques to unlock malted barley's hidden treasures. The next chapter dives into the magic of mashing and its pivotal role in extracting fermentable sugars for wort production. But first, let us pause to appreciate malted barley's rich flavors waiting to emerge through the brewer's alchemy.

The Magic of Mashing

With high-quality malt, the brewer's next step unleashes its stellar potential through mashing. Here, malt meets hot water to dissolve sugars, proteins, and other compounds essential for fermentation. Manipulating time, temperatures, and chemistry during the mash gives the brewer control over wort character and alcohol yield. Though intricate in theory, basic mashing requires no more than a pot, filter, thermometer, and some elbow grease.

Mashing stages unfold throughout a one to two-hour steeping process targeting specific temperature plateaus. Strike water, heated twenty degrees higher than the target temp, almost instantly drops upon hitting the grain. After an initial rapid drop, the mash stabilizes quickly within a few degrees of the target. Monitoring and stirring help avoid over or under-shooting rest points. It is too low, and starch conversion lags while enzyme denaturing spikes near 170°F. Throughout all stages, the brewer constantly checks temperature and textures.

Though water alone suffices, advanced mashing regimes amplify chemistry and results. Mineral additions or acidification in the strike water counteract pH levels from the grains. Mashes tend to be alkaline, so brewers add gypsum, calcium chloride, phosphoric acid, or lactic acid to stabilize pH at the zone's optimal 5.2 to 5.6 sweet spot. Chemistry maximizes enzymatic output and wort clarity. Savvy brewers build staggered multi-step procedures to target specific enzymes and flavor profiles over the hour.

Just as each ingredient and technique builds upon the other to form harmony, mashing all comes together in service of yeast, flavor, and control. Vessel by vessel, from germination to glass, liquid, and process, honor those yeast strands that turn wort's hidden nectar into beer.

The Magic Starts at Doughing-In

The best start rests upon accurately measuring out grains and striking water. With proper amounts, hitting target temperatures and thickness becomes possible. Weight ratios simplify calculations for the homebrewer since most grain absorption rates hover around one quart absorbed per pound. Commercial systems rely on computer controls and flow meters.

Grist preparation also proves vital for efficiency and lautering. Grist refers to the coarse crush applied to malt kernels by rotating metal rollers at the mill. Gaping cracks multiply surface area to better release starches without excessively pulverizing them into flour. Over-milled grist complicates sparging and sticks in pipes, while under-milled grain limits output. Finding the optimal crush only comes from careful calibration and testing.

With equipment prepared and grist precisely weighed, brewers measure out the initial liquor charge into the mash tun. Liquor refers to any water used for steeping grains or sparging, regardless of mineral additions. As the vessel heats the liquor, the pale, chocolate, roasted, or crystal malts stand at the ready, grouped by recipe. This staged positioning assists doughing-in once strike temperature hits the target by prioritizing base malts' contact with liquor. Careful doughing-in by hand or mechanical mixer ensures clump elimination and temperature consistency.

Now officially a mash, the thick porridge ticks down through enzymes awakening. Constant checks track the gradual temperature slides and plateau at teaching degree points. As the brewer nurtures the mash, the starches dissolve, chains split, and the wort comes into one glucose unit at a time. Subtly sweet tones emerge, signaling the enzymes' landmark achievements.

Protein Rests: Reducing Haze Factors

Transitioning a one-step infusion mash to a stepped regimen targets specific enzymatic activity windows through temperature adjustments. By moving through progressively higher rests, multi-step profiles extend starch conversion, then cell wall breakdown, and finally, sugar formation, finishing with a raised mash-out rest.

Brewers often start this staircase by briefly dipping into the zone just below starch gelatinization from 113° to 135°F to relax grain husks. A protein rest coagulates higher temperature haze instigators, improving downstream clarity. The protein coagulation and degradation peaks hover between 122° and 135°F, respectively. By keeping rests brief, brewhouses maximize precipitant formation while avoiding lighter compounds dissolving back into the wort later.

Leveling protein and tannin content too aggressively strips out head retention components and diminishes the body. For less hopped German lagers, brewmasters push higher into protein reduction to finish crisp and bright. Belgian ales favor more protein carryover, contributing to their signature hazes and lacing foam rings. Finding the proper protein rest for the beer remains a delicate balance of ideals and ingredients.

Making Impossible Sugars Possible Through Beta Glucan Rests

Malted barley contains carbohydrates from simple sugars to elaborate bonded chains—enzyme performance limits which fractions get chopped into fermentable sizes or remain longer. Cooler initial rests target sticky beta-glucans, complicating sparge filtration.

By first dipping into the 95° to 113°F zone for fifteen to twenty minutes, proteases tackle structural carbohydrates that combine barley cellulose strands with proteins. These gluey meshes inhibit wort separation and slow runoff. A beta glucan rest substantially reduces viscosity later at vorlauf.

The performance here combines temperature with timing, unlike protein precipitation. Peak activation of beta-glucanase arrives around 104°F but overspends the enzyme reserves in this bracket. Lowering closer to 95°F sustains hydrolysis across the entire rest, achieving higher overall breakdown before ramping upwards.

Though barley glucans require gelatinization over 140°F to fully dissolve, a profound beta glucan reduction makes for a smooth lautering. Brewers producing Belgian ambers or German bocks likely skip this step, tolerating the Beer hazes. Hoppy session beers demand more attention on runoff clarity.

Mashing Maximization Reigns During Starch Conversion
Ascending upward again, the now more apparent wort bath approaches the alpha and beta amylase happy place bracket from 140° to 160°F for saccharification. This third rest zone focuses on starch conversion into fermentable through distinct enzyme pathways. Alpha amylase chews raw starch chains rapidly into glucose and maltose but denatures past 168°F, rendering it useless. Beta amylase activities generate more sucrose and long maltochains on the flavor side, contributing to a slick-mouth feel.

Finding the suitable duration and temperature balance to maximize fermentability involves understanding enzyme kinetics. While both amylase pathways operate across the gelatinization spectrum from 140° to 170°F, their peak productivity diverges. Alpha amylase rapidly fires on all cylinders when temperatures hit 158° to 162°F if held there for forty-five to seventy minutes. In contrast, beta amylase chugs away at only half speed in this same range while peaking closer to the limit of its thermostability at 148°F.

Juggling both effects leads most single infusion brewers to split the difference with a saccharification rest around 154°F for sixty minutes, satisfying moderate starch breakdown. High adjunct recipes push slightly upward, chasing more fermentability from the alpha-amylase side. Step-mash regimens often tackle lower and higher brackets, pursuing the best of both worlds.

No matter whether infusion or multi-step, only brewers finish a mash nowadays with a seventy-five degree Celsius rest. This enzyme denaturing prelude to lautering ensures no further starch conversion during sparging. By heating to around 170°F, alpha and beta amylase permanently deactivate, avoiding unwanted residual sweetness in packaging. After hitting mash-out temps, continual stirring keeps the grain bed stable ahead of vorlauf and sparge.

With sugars maximized and enzymes denatured, the foundation wort unlocks from the grains during vorlauf and lautering. Further steps await bittering, flavoring, and fermentation guided by old friends' hops and yeast. Before diving into their contributions, let us pause and toast malt, the backbone of all beers. Salut!

Lautering Loses the Grains and Clarifies the Wort
They are crossing the finish line of mashing hands, the baton off to lautering for separating and rinsing the sweet wort away from grains. Here, gravity filtration through the grain bed and incremental sparging washes residual sugars into the boil kettle. While lautering sounds simple, the devil hides in the details of avoiding a stuck runoff or channeling.

Preparing for the transfer starts with verification of mash conversion completeness through an iodine test. A few drops on a spoonful sample will maintain amber colors when starches wash away, indicating a sugar-rich wort primed for runoff. Conversely, green or indigo iodine staining reveals an unfinished saccharification requiring more steeping time. With conversion validated, vorlauf commences re-circulating cloudy infused liquor from beneath the grain basket before directing flow into the kettle.

Stirring up sediment during this deceptively named "pre-runoff" accelerates grain bed settling while forming natural filter channels through husk particulates. Continual recirculation wears down larger particles and loosens sticky mashes ahead of sparging. Clarity noticeably improves from hazy to translucent, signaling the transition to open up direct drainage. Vorlauf's duration runs ten to twenty minutes or more for high adjunct recipes prone to clogging down the line.

With pathways cleared, sparging commences the gradual top-down application of hot water for rinsing additional sugars. The thin syrupy liquid passing the grain bed extraction efficiency spikes briefly up from seventy percent range towards eighty-plus percent. Careful measurements dictate strike and sparge amounts for hitting target pre-boil volumes with calculated losses afterward.

The increasing hypotonic runnings simultaneously thin from the grain bed, draining sugars until a point of diminishing returns. By monitoring with a refractometer, the degree Plato steadily drops from around seven to one or two over seventy-five to ninety minutes of runoff. Brewers end sparging rather than leeching harsh tannins at this faded straw color, signifying most fermentables collected. What remains gets repurposed for cleaning or irrigation, fulfilling the zero-waste brewer ideal. While lautering may seem an unglamorous middle step, mastery over sparging provides the brewer great control over their vision. Building a thirst-worthy wort chock full of enzymes and nutrition prepares an optimal playground for yeast to create magic. Bittering, flavoring, and fermentation depend on a healthy wort foundation.

With sugar-rich wort now transferred into the brew kettle, the open palette welcomes hops and yeast to bring their potent magic. First,

those aromatic cones from bine vines bitter and spice the purified runoff ahead
Of active fermentation. Let us next explore the wonders of hop alchemy!

Chapter 3

Hops: Nature's Beer Spice

What are Hops and Why Are They Used in Beer?

As you sip an IPA bursting with tropical fruit and pine aromas or a balanced blonde ale with a touch of floral spice, you likely have never stopped to ponder - what exactly are these "hops" that impart such dynamic flavors and bouquets to beer? This chapter will unveil everything you need to know about these overlooked ingredients and why they are pivotal in producing the diverse beer styles enjoyed globally.

When hops meet malt and yeast in the brewing process, magic happens. Hops are the spice that balance the sweetness of malt and elevate the fermented beverage into something ethereal. Botanically classified as Humulus lupulus, the hop plant is a bine (a climbing plant that grows on other plants or structures for support, unlike vines, which use tendrils) in the Cannabaceae family, closely related to another infamous member of that group - cannabis. While hops won't deliver the psychoactive high associated with marijuana, they can undoubtedly provide drinkers with an equally intoxicating experience through their contributions to beer.

Hops grow well in temperate climates with decent sunlight and require structures to wrap their bines around as they grow vertically between 10 to 25 feet high. Major hop production regions include Germany, China, the USA, Australia, and New Zealand. The hop plants produce cone-shaped flowers that house the precious, aromatic yellow lupulin glands so coveted by brewers. These glands contain the majority of flavor and aroma compounds provided by hops. The extracts derived from these glands through hop processing lend beer qualities described as citrusy, piney, floral, herbal, spicy, or even tropical fruity when used in beer.

So why are hops a non-negotiable ingredient for quality beer? For starters, the bitterness delivered by hops balances the sweetness from malted barley, allowing for more drinkability and attenuation. Hops also have a mild preservative effect, helping to protect the final product from spoilage and provide stability. Most importantly, hops add complexity to beer, elevating it beyond just sugary water through dynamic flavors and bouquets. By thoughtfully selecting certain hop varieties and judiciously determining addition timings in the brewing process, brewers can fine-tune bitterness perception, flavor contributions, and aromatic essence in their beer to achieve the exact profile envisioned for the style.

The essential compounds driving hops' bittering perception, flavor, and aroma are iso-alpha acids, polyphenols, and essential oils. These compounds vary substantially between different hop cultivars. Bittering potential is assessed by examining the alpha acid percentage of a given hop variety. Top hop varieties for bittering include Magnum, Nugget, Chinook, and Simcoe, all with alpha acid levels above 12%. Flavor hop darlings feature reasonably high levels of polyphenols to stimulate taste buds effectively and include Mt. Hood, Crystal, Centennial, and Amarillo varieties. Finally, aroma hop celebrities relied on to impart beguiling bouquets containing concentrated essential oils. Citra, Galaxy, Mosaic, Vic Secret, and Nelson Sauvin are prime examples.

By thoughtfully combining bittering, flavor, and aroma hop varieties throughout critical points in the brewing production, craft brewers expertly conduct a hop symphony to achieve stunning flavor and aroma crescendos in their India Pale Ales while also using restrained hopping rates for subtle nobility in English Bitters. Some classic combinations include Cascade/Centennial for American IPAs to yield citrus overload, Amarillo/Simcoe for a tropical fruit explosion, or East Kent Goldings/Fuggles for the quintessential English ale experience.

Hops can be utilized in various forms throughout the brewing process to impart their magic touch, including:
- Whole flower hops - Plump cones added directly to the boiling wort or fermentation tank
- Pellet hops - Milled and compressed cones forming condensed pellets for concentrated compounds
- Hop extract - Concentrated distillate used for intense flavor/aroma additions without vegetal matter

No matter what form the hops take in beer creation, these wondrous flowers provide the seasoning touch that takes fermented malt beverages from ho-hum to holes-in-your-socks Humulus lupulus deliciousness! While the lovable yeast beasts do the hard work of fermentation and alcohol production in beer, hops are their most glamorous ingredient - bringing personality, nuance, and depth to beers. From noble Saaz delicacy to aggressive CTZ dankness and everything in between, hops inject aromas, flavors, and bitterness indispensable in the alchemy of outstanding ales and lagers!

With this foundation on the role of hops established, in the next chapter on yeast, we will uncover how those tiny unicellular fungi work their magic through fermentation to transform sugary wort into effervescent, alcoholic beer!

Growing Hops - From Propagation to Harvest

The exponential rise of craft brewing has fueled a newfound fascination with locality as brewers aim to source regional ingredients to highlight distinct geographic terroir. As hops provide such a pivotal trademark for many signature beer styles, a key point of distinction becomes showcasing uniquely expressive hops grown in one's backyard. Backyard hops endeavors have exploded in popularity with gardening hobbyists and brewers cultivating bines in their gardens or hop fields for neighborhood harvests. If you are lucky enough to live in hop-friendly climates like the Pacific Northwest, USA, New Zealand, or central Europe, local artisan hops fresh off the bine infuse unique character into brews.

Yet just because you may call a region without an ideal hop-growing climate home doesn't mean you should despair about incorporating home-sourced hops into beers. Passionate hobby gardeners across less temperate zones are finding success planting potted hop rhizomes that climb lattices, trellises, or fences. Techniques like strategic pruning, proper watering, pest prevention, and moving potted bine indoors during harsh weather allow domestic hop cultivation spanning USDA Hardiness Zones 3-9. When harvest rolls around, these homegrown hops find their noble purpose for existence during a celebratory backyard fresh hop beer brewed as a badge of gardening honor amongst friends.

So how exactly does one propagate and pamper budding hop bines into mature cones ready for brew day glory? Once the final frost passes, you should procure hearty rhizomes or nursery starter plants in early spring. Focus on securing quality rootstock from reputable sources of cultivars suited for your latitude. Vital options include Cascade, Centennial, Chinook, Nugget, or Crystal for reliable yields. Next, identify a planting area with decent sunlight, proper drainage, and support structure access, such as a fence or established trellis between 10 to 18 feet high. Amend native soil by digging 1 foot down, mixing in rich compost or aged manure, then backfilling planting holes with improved soil. Space multiple rhizomes 2 to 3 feet apart to allow each bine room to spread. Plant rhizomes horizontally just 1 to 2 inches underground, keeping the growth buds pointing up. Water thoroughly, then mulch around new plantings.

As green shoots emerge from underground rhizomes in late spring, train the fledgling bines clockwise around supports. Utilize soft plant ties to secure stems gently on every foot without restricting vascular flows. Maintain moist soil as bines rapidly elongate, seeking sunlight. Monitor for pest invaders like spider mites or Japanese beetles and take appropriate organic measures to control infestations. Supply supplemental nitrogen by working-aged manure or pelletized chicken manure into topsoil and mulch layers monthly through the summer growing season. Keep weeds suppressed to minimize soil pathogens and nuisance competition. Strategically pinch off wayward bines, allowing 3 to 4 vigorous vines to scale supports while redirecting energy toward flower development. Staking individual flowering side arms prevents breakage when heavy with ripe cones. Come late summer, ethanol aromas will hint at lupulin readiness!

Judge peak ripeness for plucking whole hop vines by noticing papery dry cone bracts, yellow lupulin dusting, and browned vines about six weeks after flower emergence. Carefully cut entire vines near soil level. Rapidly strip cones off bines, discard sticks and leaves, then place fresh hops into breathable harvest bags for refrigerated storage. Utilize fresh hops within 24 hours by drying, freezing, or brewing to prevent deterioration. Alternatively, kiln-dried whole cone hops retain beneficial compounds when vacuum sealed and then frozen for subsequent seasons.

With basic propagation principles covered, backyard hop hobbyists can gain respectable small-scale yields of 30 to 40 dried cones per healthy rhizome. Harvesting pounds of flowers is realistic with acres of hop trellising! However, the real treasure exists in producing unique wet hop beer showcasing the exceptional local terroir your homegrown hops imbibe based on soil constitution, ambient yeast populations, and regional climate fluctuations. So, just a few handfuls of fresh cones can contribute signature essence and bragging rights to fresh hopped ales amongst homebrewing circles!

The Art and Science of Hop Additions in Beer Production

Now that fledgling flowers have been coaxed into cone fruition via backyard bounty or commercial crops, how do brewers harness the bittering, flavor, and aromatic compounds during critical points along the brewing continuum?

The valued acids, oils, and polyphenols within hops dock onto proteins and sugars in the boiling kettle, forming new compounds that impart bitterness, flavor, and eventually aromatics into beer. By thoughtfully staggering additions based on solubility, desired isomerization, and biotransformation reactions influenced by duration and temperature exposures, brewers conduct a hop rollercoaster, strategically plateauing and cascading passengers along each phase from mash to fermentation.

The first station involves getting in line to board the bitterness train! Brewers achieve clean, pleasant bitterness by introducing higher alpha hop varieties early in the boil when vigorous convection allows efficient isomerization, converting soluble alpha acids into iso-alpha acids. These newly minted iso-alpha acids are less chemically stable and persist without degradation during stressful boiling. Iso-alpha acids survive the subsequent fermentation gauntlet to enable perceived bitterness when sipped. Magnum, Horizon, Bravo, and Warrior represent classic high alpha acids. Charging down the first hills of the rollercoaster ride generates exciting bursts of hoppy flavor next! Mid-boil additions between 20-5 minutes left utilize progenitor hop varieties with robust polyphenol levels that biotransform during partial isomerization into oxidized derivatives. These activating reactions enable more robust neurological taste bud responses than aroma compounds alone. Noteworthy hop choices for flavor popping include Crystal, Apollo, Columbus, and Simcoe varieties.

As the boiling brew transitions from turbulent rapids into a peaceful fermentation sea, the final hop coaster hills deliver enveloping hop perfume effortlessly across the surface without volatile oil degradation from harsh boil temperatures. Whirlpooling hop stand additions after flameout impart initial hop essence as organics extract from vegetal matter while the wort rests. Even more profound aromas emerge from end-stage dry hopping after primary fermentation ceases since the bioconversion of hop compounds during active yeast metabolism amplifies overall hoppiness perception in finished beers. Sed for a bittering charge. Magnum, Horizon, Bravo, and Warrior represent classic high alpha acid powerhouses favored for clean bitterness contributions without flavor distraction.

Charging down the first hills of the rollercoaster ride generates exciting bursts of hoppy flavor next! Mid-boil additions between 20-5 minutes left utilize progenitor hop varieties with robust polyphenol levels that biotransform during partial isomerization into oxidized derivatives. These activating reactions enable more robust neurological taste bud responses than aroma compounds alone. Noteworthy hop choices for flavor popping include Crystal, Apollo, Columbus, and Simcoe varieties.

As the boiling brew transitions from turbulent rapids into a peaceful fermentation sea, the final hop coaster hills deliver enveloping hop perfume effortlessly across the surface without volatile oil degradation from harsh boil temperatures. Whirlpooling hop stand additions after flameout impart initial hop essence as organics extract from vegetal matter while the wort rests. Even more profound aromas emerge from end-stage dry hopping after primary fermentation ceases since the bioconversion of hop compounds during active yeast metabolism amplifies overall hoppiness perception in finished beers.

Hops, Malt, Yeast, and Water

Chapter 4

Yeast: Tiny Beasts That Make Beer

No ingredient is more important to beer than yeast. Yeast's ability to consume sugars and create alcohol and carbon dioxide forms the biological engine driving fermentation and beer's signature effervescence. Getting to know these microscopic fungi on a deeper level unlocks the full flavor potential of your homebrew.

While usually invisible to the naked eye, yeast cells teem by the billions in fermentation tanks. Under the microscope, these single-cell spheres, ovals, or elongated capsules drift lazily about. Some yeasts link together, forming distinct clumps or flocs to help the yeast sediment out of the finished beer. Their seeming simplicity hides surprising complexity within.

Yeast Biology 101

Despite their tiny size—barely large enough to be seen by the human eye—yeast cells contain all the essential machinery of life. Like bacteria, yeast belongs to the scientific "kingdoms" of protists or fungi, straddling the boundary between both groups. Possessing distinct nuclei containing genetic material, cell membranes, proteins, enzymes, ribosomes, mitochondria, and other specialized cell components, yeast efficiently convert sugar into cellular energy and reproduce via cell division and budding of daughter cells.

While all yeast shares basic similarities, hundreds of specialized strains have evolved in nature over millions of years. Brewers exploit this genetic diversity to produce distinct beer styles. Ale yeast ferments warm and briskly, retaining fruity esters and flavors. Lager strains require cooler temperatures, cleanly fermenting away residuals that might cause off-flavors. Within these broad categories, individual strains impart specific characteristics detected in the final brew.

The Yeast Life Cycle

Yeast reproduction follows a rapid, predictable pattern through the cell cycle phases. Resting cells transition from dormancy into a growth phase upon introduction to the wort, the sweet liquid extracted from mashed grain that yeast ferment into beer. Energized by their banquet, single parent cells asymmetrically divide into more giant daughter cells, which continue budding exponentially.

A frenzy of metabolic activity and cell division follows during the first 72 hours of fermentation, with a typical doubling time of 90 to 180 minutes under optimal conditions. Yeast colonies can thus mushroom from a few million cells to over 100 billion in just a few days! Tracking this explosive growth phase helps schedule key processes like transferring the beer or adding fruit or ingredients.

As fermentable sugars diminish and alcohol concentrations build, yeast shifts from reproduction to maintenance and survival. Daughter cells form but do not separate, remaining embedded in mature parents. Clumps and sediment begin accumulating at the bottom of the fermenter. When all sugars are exhausted, metabolism grinds to a halt, and the yeast converts to a hibernating state until roused by the next infusion of sweet wort or priming sugar to carbonate the finished beer.

While the above captures the essence of S. cerevisiae behavior, the exact details depend greatly on specific strains and fermentation conditions like sugar levels and temperature, oxygenation, level of pitching, and many other factors explored later in this book. Master brewers learn to carefully control fermentation by understanding what makes their yeast tick!

Energy Production and Metabolism

Like all living organisms, yeast requires cellular energy sources to grow and reproduce. The microbes have evolved specialized internal structures and complex metabolic pathways to harvest energy locked within sugars via oxidation reactions. This aerobic respiration neatly breaks down food within the cell, unlike anaerobic fermentation, which incompletely digests sugars without oxygen.

The first steps involve intricate protein complexes on the cell membrane that actively transport simple sugars like glucose or fructose using ion gradients. Once inside, additional proteins and enzymes break down these sugars stepwise through glycolysis metabolic pathways featuring many intermediate compounds. The energy released at each step eventually feeds into the Krebs cycle and an electron transport chain within the mitochondria, which combines the sugars with oxygen to unlock carbon dioxide, water, and adenosine triphosphate molecules used throughout cells as an energy transfer mechanism. This marathon sprint powers all other cell activity.

When oxygen runs low amid active fermentation, yeast instead undergo alcohol fermentation, which converts sugar first to pyruvate acid and finally into ethanol and carbon dioxide gas, making up the hearty foam crowning your favorite pint! This less efficient process leaves behind desirable flavors and aromas but provides only two ATP molecules per glucose molecule, limiting yeast growth. Many byproducts like glycerol, acids, esters, phenols, and fusel alcohols also emerge, contributing to the beer's final profile.

This overview just touches on the rich complexity of yeast metabolism. Their inner workings depend significantly on environmental factors like nutrition, osmotic pressure, alcohol toxicity, temperature extremes, or fluctuations during fermentation. As craft brewers better understand yeast biology under varied conditions, they can better tweak their processes towards desired outcomes.

Chapter 5

Water Chemistry and Adjustments

Understanding Water: The Foundation of Great Beer

As a homebrewer, you likely obsess over ingredients like malted barley, hops, and yeast—seeking out the freshest, most flavorful varieties to create your signature brews. But there's one ingredient that often gets overlooked: water. After all, it seems simple enough to use tap water or filter it to remove chlorine and impurities. However, water chemistry plays a critical role in brewing. Ion concentrations, pH, and mineral profiles impact mash efficiency, yeast health, enzyme activity, and finished beer flavor. Understanding water and making adjustments can elevate your homebrew to the next level.

When I first started homebrewing, I didn't think much about my water. It was OK to run tap water through a carbon filter and use that. My early brews turned out drinkable, but nothing remarkable. When I started analyzing my water and tweaking it, the flavors began popping. Adjusting sulfate and chloride ions boosted hop expression or maltiness precisely how I wanted. Getting the mash pH right improved efficiency and fermentability. Building customized profiles for classic beer styles took them from ho-hum to fantastic. Water is the foundation of all beer, carrying the most significant imprint on the final flavor. Once I realized that, it became a key focus rather than an afterthought.

The Science Behind Water Chemistry

Before adjusting your brewing water, it helps to understand what's in there and why it matters. Water contains various mineral ions, some beneficial, some not so much. Essential ions for brewing include calcium, magnesium, sodium, sulfate, chloride, bicarbonate, carbonate, and silicate. The concentrations and ratios of these ions influence mash chemistry, yeast health, enzyme activity, hop extraction, and finished flavor. Water also has pH, which impacts mash efficiency and fermentation. We'll dig into all of this more below.

Starting with minerals, calcium is essential for brewing. It promotes precise break formation in the boil, drives yeast health, and aids enzyme activity in the mash. Magnesium helps regulate those enzymatic processes. Sodium can enhance flavor perception but goes a long way, so a little makes a big difference.

Some ions play a crucial role in influencing beer style and flavor characteristics. Sulfate accentuates hop bitterness, so increased levels help craft intensely bitter and dry IPAs. Chloride enhances malt flavors and creates a round, full mouthfeel—higher chloride suits English bitters and porters. Finding the proper sulfate-to-chloride ratio for a style makes a noticeable difference.

Carbonate and bicarbonate ions affect mash pH. They make water more alkaline, reducing extract efficiency in the mash and inhibiting yeast during fermentation. Most brewing water needs downward pH adjustments using acid. However, highly acidic water can be problematic, too, so you need to land in the sweet spot: around 5.2 to 5.6 mash pH, depending on the style.

Now, where does this medley of ions come from exactly? Some originate in the geology and environment from which the water is sourced. Mineral content varies widely across reservoirs, rivers, lakes, and underground aquifers based on surrounding rock. Municipal water authorities also add chemicals during treatment, such as chlorine, fluoride, lime, and soda ash—all of which influence ion levels. And that's before it even gets to your house! Further filtration and chemical treatment from your tap water filter continue altering the mineral balance.

No two water supplies have the same makeup; it's a chemical melting pot when it hits your brew kettle. The key is understanding what's in your starting water to customize adjustments for making great beer with your water's signature.

Reading a Water Report

Thankfully, municipal water authorities test and publish consumer confidence reports detailing exactly what's in your tap water. You can find these reports online by searching "<Your City> water quality report." For example, I found my local Tucson report at Tucsonaz.gov/water. These reports contain a table listing all detected minerals, their parts per million (ppm) concentrations, and water pH and hardness. Essential brewing ions like calcium, chloride, sulfate, carbonate, bicarbonate, sodium, magnesium, and silica will be listed. It's a goldmine of intel for brewing chemistry geeks!

Analyzing these values against known style guidelines provides guidance on which minerals to adjust up or down and by how much. For example, Tucson water contains 140ppm bicarbonate, making it more alkaline. Most beer styles call for lower pH mash water, around 5.2-5.6. Some acid addition will be required to neutralize excess bicarbonate and reduce alkalinity to get there. We'll cover making these adjustments shortly.

First, what do those fundamental ion values mean for your beer? Here's a quick guide:

Calcium: 50-150ppm desired
Accentuates hop bitterness; enhances clarity and flavor; drives yeast health.

Magnesium: 10-30ppm desired
Supports enzymatic processes; contributes to flavor complexity

Sodium: 0-150ppm
Enhances flavor perception at low levels; becomes harsh above 150ppm

Sulfate: 50-800ppm+
Accentuates hop flavors; very high levels suit IPAs

Chloride: 0-300ppm
Enhances malt character and full mouthfeel; boosts English styles.

Carbonate: 0-50ppm
Increases pH/alkalinity; usually needs downward adjustment

Bicarbonate: 0-150ppm
Increases pH/alkalinity; usually needs downward adjustment

Silica: Less than 10ppm
Prevents scale buildup in equipment at low levels

Now, let's move on to making adjustments!

Adjusting Alkalinity with Acid

Looking again at my Tucson water report, the exceptionally high 140ppm bicarbonate immediately sticks out. This makes the water quite alkaline, with a pH around eight coming out of the tap. But most beer styles need a mash pH between 5.2 and 5.6 for optimal extraction and conversion.

Brewers add food-grade acid to neutralize excess carbonate and bicarbonate ions to reduce that alkalinity. Standard brewing acid options include lactic, phosphoric, nitric, sulfuric, citric, or acidulated malt in the mash.

Phosphoric acid works exceptionally well to target mash pH in small 0.1-0.5ml additions. It neutralizes carbonate and lowers mash pH consistently without adding flavor. I dose phosphoric acid in my brewing liquor until reaching my desired mash pH based on style. For ales, I shoot for pH 5.2-5.4 and lagers pH 5.4-5.6.

Using popular brewing water calculators, one can quickly estimate acid needs (Bru'n Water, Brewer's Friend, EZ Water Calculator). Simply input your starting water chemistry, grains, and batch size, and it suggests acid additions to hit your pH goal. Dial in amounts based on actual pH meter readings during the mash. Voila! Dialed-in water chemistry.

Now, don't confuse water pH with beer pH; they are entirely different! We adjust our water to mash at 5.2-5.6 pH to ensure optimal conversion and extraction. However, the finished beer's pH is around 4.1-4.5 thanks to new organic acid production during fermentation. Water pH adjustments impact beer flavor but aren't responsible for final pH.

Building Water Profiles

In addition to adjusting alkalinity, we can build specific ion profiles suited to beer styles using mineral salt additions. Hulls, sulfates, and chlorides all influence character.

Boosting sulfate accentuates crisp hop bitterness. Chloride enhances malt body and residual sweetness. Ratios vary widely across styles, from bitter, dry West Coast IPAs to malty English ales. Maximizing these contributions makes a difference you can taste.

Desired minerals get added directly to brewing liquor as salts. Common options include gypsum (calcium sulfate), Epsom salts (magnesium sulfate), calcium chloride, and sodium chloride (table salt). Weigh additions according to style guidelines and water chemistry software. For example:

West Coast IPA
Sulfate: 400-800 ppm
Chloride: up to 300 ppm
Desired sulfate-to-chloride ratio 4:1

English Bitter
Sulfate: 300-500 ppm
Chloride: 200-300 ppm
Desired sulfate-to-chloride ratio 1:1

I adjust sulfate, chloride, and sodium minerals in the brewing water to complement the dominant malt or hop character I seek. Significant additions aren't necessary if your water already contains adequate minerals. However building a specific profile makes a tremendous difference in tasting the impact of ions. My hoppy pale ale completely transforms using the sulfate boost!

Removing Unwanted Minerals

Sometimes, water contains excess minerals that require removal before brewing instead of addition. This occurs primarily with chlorine/chloramine from municipal treatment, iron, manganese, sulfur compounds, zinc, copper, fluoride, and sodium.

Chlorine/chloramine demand elimination via chemical treatment or charcoal filtration. Iron, manganese, sulfur, and zinc also require pre-removal as they contribute to off-flavors. High sodium levels make beer salty, limiting its use for brewing unless diluted with cleaner sources.

Common pre-removal tactics include:

- Activated carbon filtration - absorbs chlorine and organics
- Reverse osmosis - removes dissolved solids
- Distillation via steam stripping - purifies through evaporation
- Ion exchange - replaces unwanted ions with preferred ones
- Dilution with cleaner water - halves concentrations

Testing your source water determines which unwanted minerals may need addressing before brewing. Their removal ensures you start adjustment from a clean, flavor-neutral slate upon which to build your favored mouthfeel and hop/malt balance.

Now that we've covered the what, why, and how behind brewing water chemistry, let's recap some key takeaways to remember as you analyze your water and tweak it to make better beer:

Water Chemistry Quick Hits

- Water makes up 90%+ of beer, providing the foundation of all flavors
- Every water source has a unique mineral profile that influences beer
- Key ions for brewing include calcium, magnesium, sodium, sulfate, chloride, carbonate & bicarbonate
- Their levels and ratios impact mash chemistry, yeast health, hop/malt expression, and final beer character
- Read your municipal water report detailing exact levels of critical minerals, pH, and hardness
- Common adjustments involve adding acid to alter mash pH and mineral salts to accentuate dry/bitter or malty qualities
- Metro tap water often has high levels of carbonate & bicarbonate, requiring acid treatment
- Target mash pH 5.2-5.6 based on style using phosphoric or lactic acid additions
- Use sulfate, calcium & sodium to boost hop-forward dryness in IPAs
- Use chloride & magnesium to enhance malt body and residual sweetness in English beers
- Remove unwanted ions like iron, manganese, sulfur, chlorine, and fluoride, which cause off-flavors
- Building custom profiles suited to beer styles makes a tremendous difference you can taste!

I wish someone had impressed me years earlier that more than simply filtering water was needed. One must understand its chemical makeup, then tweak alkalinity, residual minerals, pH, etc, to match the desired beer profile. It took me years to realize correctly treating brewing water was such low-hanging fruit for dramatically better beer with little effort!

Now that you understand the same apply these lessons to analyze your brewing water chemistry and make simple adjustments. I guarantee it takes whatever beer you're driving to the next level! Thirsty work makes the first glass taste even sweeter once you brew water with purpose. The next round's on me!

Optimizing Water Chemistry By Style

Now that we've covered the fundamentals of brewing water, understanding your starting profile, and making basic adjustments—let's take a deep dive into building custom water treatments optimized for different beer styles.

As discussed earlier, specific ions have signature effects enhancing hoppy, bitter characteristics or malty, full qualities. We can strategically boost these mineral contributors to complement the overall style we wish to brew. I'll share my tailored water profiles for crafting iconic styles from dry hop-bursts to roasty stouts. Follow my templates here or tweak mineral amounts to your preference once you grasp the impact of each ion.

When developing custom water profiles, we first gather details on our untreated starting water supply—which, for this example, we'll assume resembles my local Tucson water makeup. Then, we adjust that base upwards or downwards with mineral salt additions to achieve our desired ion levels for the planned beer style. Here's a quick look at our baseline untreated water composition:

Tucson Untreated Water Profile

Calcium: 70ppm
Magnesium: 24ppm

Sodium: 100ppm
Sulfate: 250ppm
Chloride: 100ppm
Carbonate: 50ppm
Bicarbonate: 140ppm
pH: 8.2

You can reference your municipal report or water testing to input your untreated water chemistry. Let's see how we'd tweak this baseline to suit some popular styles!

Hoppy West Coast IPA

We want to maximize sulfate content to craft an aromatic, dry, and massively hopped West Coast IPA to make those hop flavors pop. This showcases classic Cali IPAs with intense bitterness, pine, and citrus notes from American hop varieties like Chinook, Centennial, Cascade, and Amarillo.

We'll add gypsum (calcium sulfate) to boost levels to 500-1000 ppm, targeting a 4:1 ratio favoring sulfate over chloride. High sulfate dries out the finish and cranks up hop perceptions. We'll brew with mostly base malts, perhaps just a dash of light caramel malt, to not compete with the bold hop statement.

Target Water Profile:
Hoppy West Coast IPA

Calcium: 180ppm
Magnesium: 24ppm
Sodium: 150ppm
Sulfate: 800ppm
Chloride: 200ppm

Carbonate: 0ppm

pH 5.3

To build this playing up sulfate while reducing carbonate, I would add 10 grams of food-grade phosphoric acid to reduce alkalinity down close to 0ppm. Then, for mineral supplementation, add 20g of gypsum and 5g of table salt to achieve the sulfate, calcium, and sodium spec provided.

The phosphoric acid needed to neutralize my Tucson water's high untreated bicarbonate levels allows me to layer on the desired flavor-boosting minerals. This takes my blank canvas water and transforms it into the quintessential dry, hoppy IPA foundation.

Crisp Kolsch-Style Ale

Transitioning from the hop assault of an IPA to the crisp, delicate balance of a Kolsch provides another fun water tweaking opportunity. This light German ale displays tangy fruit esters, soft grainy malt sweetness, and restrained bitterness around 25-35 IBUs.

I like targeting equal levels of sulfate and chloride ions around 150-200 ppm to play up this subtle interplay while keeping the beer crisp and drinkable. This showcases the refined malt flavors without letting hops dominate the palate. I'll also boost calcium to 100ppm to aid clarity and filterability—which is essential for this classic style.

Target Water Profile:

Kolsch-Style Ale

Calcium: 100ppm

Magnesium: 24ppm

Sodium: 75ppm

Sulfate: 175ppm

Chloride: 175ppm

Carbonate: 0ppm
pH 5.4

Achieving this calls for adding 5g calcium chloride and 10g calcium sulfate (gypsum), plus phosphoric acid to reduce carbonate alkalinity. This gives a beautifully balanced mouthfeel, neither rich nor bitter—perfect for crushing a few cold ones!

Malty English Brown Ale

For malt-focused English brown ales, porters, and sweet stouts, we want to do the opposite of hoppy IPAs and boost that soft, bready, caramel malt deliciousness. Chloride is our friend here to create a fuller body and lingering sweetness.

We'll only lightly bitter these roasty styles around 15-25 IBUs, letting dark malts like chocolate and black patent provide most of the flavor. Some subtle fruit esters fermenting in the mid-60s °F help bring additional complexity. Our chloride-heavy water profile gives a luscious texture and sweetness, staying true to the style.

Target Water Profile:
English Brown Ale

Calcium: 150ppm
Magnesium: 24ppm
Sodium: 75ppm
Sulfate: 200ppm
Chloride: 300ppm
Carbonate: 25ppm
pH 5.3

To translate our untreated Tucson water into these parameters, I'd add a bit of acid to gently reduce carbonate while driving up calcium and chloride ions with 5g of calcium chloride and 5g of gypsum additions.

This gives a beautiful chemistry blank canvas to create rich, malty sweetness painting in this style's specialty dark grains and caramel malts. The water fits like a velvet glove around the malt, smoothing out finishes and lingering on the senses.

Now that you see strategies for tailoring water mineral profiles to key beer styles, you can apply the same logic to craft any signature brew. Hoppy pale ales need a sulfate spike, just like West Coast IPAs. Belgian ales replicate the calcium-rich waters of Wallonia to aid clarity. Pilsners need soft water to let the delicate Moravian malts and Saaz hops shine.

Adjusting your brewing liquor 10-20% towards one of these profiles makes a noticeable difference. Once you grasp the art and science behind building custom water treatments, you open creative possibilities to take new recipes in original directions.

Target Mash pH By Style

Another vital water parameter to optimize when designing profiles for different beer styles is mash pH. As previously covered, mash pH affects enzyme activity, tannin extraction issues, and extraction efficiency into our sweet wort. Each style has an ideal pH range to maximize its character.

Generally, lighter beers work best in the lower 5.2-5.4 range, while darker beers and those emphasizing malt complexity drift higher around 5.5-5.7 without hitting 5.8, where tannin extraction becomes problematic. Here are some style specifics:

Hoppy Pale Ales: pH 5.2-5.3
IPAs: pH 5.2-5.4
Amber Ales: pH 5.3-5.5
Porters: pH 5.5-5.6
Stouts: pH 5.5-5.7
Sour Beers: pH 5.3-5.5

Hitting the optimal mark for your recipe means properly adjusting alkalinity in the brewing water with acid. Use phosphoric, nitric, or lactic acid additions to reduce mash pH without flavor impact.

Target the middle pH listed for the style and validate with your calibrated pH meter once the liquor and grist are combined for at least 5 minutes. Make tiny 0.2 to 0.5 ml incremental acid dosings until the desired pH is reached. This fine-tuning approach prevents overshooting your mark.

Adhering to these narrow style guidelines for mash pH makes a huge difference in maximizing conversion efficiency, yield into the fermenter and overall quality of your homebrew. It directly impacts the beer canvas and the vibrant colors you can paint!

Advanced Water Manipulation
Now that we've progressed from essential water understanding to building profiles and optimizing mouthfeel, hop/malt balance, and mash chemistry—I'd be remiss without mentioning some wizard-level advanced water techniques.

Once you become genuinely obsessed, push full geek mode on brewing water; there are almost no limits to customization. Some extreme tweaks include:

- Dilution with reverse osmosis or distilled water to reduce mineral loads for super soft Pilsners
- Acid washing dark grains the night before brewing to replicate historic highly acidic London Porter water
- Adding food-grade powdered chalk (calcium carbonate) to very soft water to boost carbonate alkalinity for Dublin stouts
- Using acid malt in grist bill to directly modify mash pH without using pure acids
- Splitting water chemistry between mash and sparge to leverage the best of both worlds
- Building the entire menu of BJCP styles by manipulating 10 gallons of distilled with mineral and acid additions
- Layering historical stone-fruit ester yeast character through calcium ion effects

Many award-winning homebrewers swear by the advanced process of splitting water treatment regimens between mash and sparge liquor. This entails creating two vastly different profiles with higher acidity and extra pale malt used in the mash to maximize efficiency and conversion pH. Then they switch to treated alkaline; high calcium sparges water to avoid tannin extraction and aid lautering drainage speed. My mind exploded, realizing how far down the water chemistry rabbit hole brewers take things to create masterpieces.

While intriguing, grasping the basics we've covered today offers enormous value in improving your beers. Start analyzing your untreated source water quality and makeup. Adjust mash pH into style-appropriate ranges with simple food-grade acid dosings. Use readily available mineral salts to incrementally shift ions towards drier hoppy bitterness or fuller rounded malt presence. Keep things simple while learning how your water responds to these tweaks over repeated brew days. Allow your palate to guide recipe adjustments based on improved perceptions. This sensory-driven feedback loop unlocks key insights no formula can teach.

Soon, you'll step back, amazed at how subtle water chemistry massages achieve bold flavor enhancements. That beautiful bitterness is popping just right. The silky mouthfeel sings with malt. Fantastic clarity and head retention reflecting happy yeast. These visible metrics manifest the water canvas optimizations underneath. Your new secret brewing weapon!

Hops, Malt, Yeast, and Water

Chapter 6

Grain to Glass: The Brewing Process

Grain to Glass: The Brewing Process

Brewing beer brings together art, science, and nature in a unique alchemical process that transforms water, malt, hops, and yeast into a delightful beverage enjoyed for millennia. We embark on a journey following the beer from its origins as seed to the final decanted glass.

Malting and Milling the Grain

Our story begins with barley, that versatile cereal grain domesticated over 10,000 years ago in the Fertile Crescent that gives beer its sweetness and body. Like most seeds, barley contains starch to feed the embryonic plant. But for brewing, the starch must first be converted to sugar that the yeast can feast upon. Through the ingenious malting process, the barley is tricked into germinating before halting it at just the right moment when the starch has turned to sugar.

The malting process starts by steeping the barley in water to absorb moisture for 2-3 days until the grain has a 42-46% moisture content. As it soaks, enzymes within the seed are activated, converting its starch stores into sugars to feed the young shoot and rootlets beginning to emerge. The wet barley is then spread out on the malting floor to germinate for around five days as the acrospire grows.

When the acrospire has grown to about 75% the length of the grain, it is plunged into a kiln heated to 60 °C to halt the germination. This crucial step captures the enzymes at their peak potency to break down starches into fermentable sugars. Too soon, and there will not be enough enzyme activity; too late, the growing plant will have consumed the sugars it made.

The final stage sees the malt kilned with hot air up to 80 °C to halt the germination and dry it again to around 4% moisture. The degree and duration of kilning also impart color and flavor compounds, from the lightest pilsners to the darkest stouts.

After malting comes milling to crack open the grain gently so that water can access and dissolve the sugars, roller mills with adjustable gaps carefully crush each kernel, scoring rather than pulverizing them. If the milling is too fine, a stuck mash can result from the floury particles clogging up the grains; it is too coarse, and the starch will be inaccessible. The perfect grind feels gritty between the fingers.

The stage is now set to mash in, mixing the milled malt with hot water to dissolve the sugars and activate the enzymes...

Mashing In and Extracting Sugars

The foundation of every beer rests in the mash - that porridge-like mixture of milled grains and hot water where sweet wort is born. As the grist is mixed with water heated to specific temperatures, the magic of enzymes unravels starch into simpler sugars that yeast can feast upon. Careful temperature control allows us to tailor wort production towards certain styles, maximizing fermentability for drier beers or leaving residual sugars for fuller bodies. We don our brewer's cap to step through the alchemical transformation within the mash.

As our crushed malt meets the hot water, the soluble proteins and sugars quickly dissolve into the liquor-like tea leaves infusing. The starch, however, remains trapped within the husks, inaccessible to the yeast on its own. Applying precise heat activates specialty enzymes that work to unzip those complex starches into smaller sugars. The enzyme beta-amylase chops the chains into maltose, while alpha-amylase creates longer maltotriose units better suited to higher-gravity beers. Too hot and they denature, too cold and they slumber. The intricate molecular dance occurs optimally between 62-72°C.

The chemistry unfolds over an hour as the liquid develops from sweet wort to sugar-rich food that the coming yeast pitch will be unable to resist. Careful temperature adjustments mid-mash let us promote certain enzymes over others and the spectrum of possible words. A single-step infusion mash lends itself well to paler, attenuated beers. The intricate multi-rest decoction mash coaxes out the maltiest doppelbock. Step mashing moves from protein rest to saccharification temperatures to make the wort more fermentable. The options for manipulation are endless.

As the magical hour ends, it is time to separate the sweet liquid gold from the spent grain through a process known as lautering. Here, the mash is transferred into a unique vessel with a false bottom that allows liquid to drain while retaining the solids. Success rests on creating a filter bed with small gaps between grain particles to form natural filtration while allowing the wort to flow. As more liquor sparges through, it rinses any remaining sugars from the grains below into the kettle.

What emerges is the elixir that makes beer possible - unfermented wort, brimming with sugars, proteins, amino acids, and flavor compounds that set the stage for each style's unique character. The grains have unlocked their secrets into the solution, yet their contribution to our craft is far from over. As we leave the mash tun behind and begin the boil, the true soul of beer begins to emerge.

Boiling and Adding Hops

As the hot wort fills the waiting kettle, the liquid unleashes its aroma into the brewery, and the true soul of this beer we are bringing into the world steps forth. The vigorous boil extracts bittering resins from hops, condenses and caramelizes the wort, precipitates excess proteins to make the beer more stable and drive off any unwanted sulfur compounds from the malt and yeast metabolism. Dialing in the boil ultimately tunes the final beer's strength, color, hop character, head retention, and clarity. Now, we step up to the brink of the steaming cauldron to guide this proto-beer through its evolution.

The boil starts by bringing our total volume of wort up to a rolling bubble, which will remain for 60 to 90 minutes, depending on the recipe. As it heats, the wort darkens slightly, concentrating as water evaporates at around 10% per hour. Unless we wish for a particularly high-gravity beer, this lost liquid is replenished with sparge water periodically. As it boils, proteins that would otherwise cause haze or instability later begin to thicken and drop out.

Hops added early in the boil contribute bitterness but little aroma, as those delicate oils vaporize if boiled for too long. So after about

30-60 minutes of protein precipitation, finishing hops are tossed in to steep and impart their enticing fruity, floral, spicy notes while minimizing further bitterness extraction. Including flavor additions, mid-boil strikes a balance to excite the drinker's interest while avoiding aggressive harshness. The hops transform pleasant, sweet wort into a lively potion unrecognizable from the first running.

As the boil nears completion, Irish moss - a type of seaweed - is introduced about 10-15 minutes from the end. The alginates from these plants attract proteins and other solids and drop them out of suspension, acting as another clarifying agent, resulting in clearer, brighter beer. If our recipe calls for any unusual additions like spices or fruit, these typically are introduced at the end of the boil or even after cooling during fermentation.

The kettle finally rests after a long boil, fragrant with hops and spice. We now turn back from the wild witch's cauldron towards the civilized kitchen as we cool this broth to ready it for the coming yeast.

Transferring, Oxygenating, and Pitching

As the rolling boil settles down and hop particulate drifts slowly like autumn leaves through the wort, the hot liquid must be quickly chilled to avoid the risk of contamination before our yeast can claim it. The faster it cools, the less risk of microbial incursion by stray bacteria or wild yeast into this sweet nectar. Rapid wort chilling also helps maximize hop aroma retention for intensely fragrant beers.

Many homebrewers start by chilling the pot in an ice bath in the sink, monitoring temperature as it plunges through the 80°C danger zone down closer to fermentation temperature. Modern breweries often use stainless steel heat exchangers to bring 5500 liters of hot wort down near freezing in half an hour! Once our broth reaches 18-22°C and we have sanitized our fermenter, we carefully siphon it out of the brew kettle, leaving much of the hop debris and coagulated proteins behind.

As the fresh wort fills our fermentation vessel, the next step is to oxygenate. Though anaerobic, brewer's yeast needs oxygen at this early stage before creating alcohol to synthesize membranes, enzymes, and other essential cell components. Ambient air has plenty for ales, but lagers require 8-10 ppm for vigorous fermentation. Brewers use aquarium pumps with sterile air filters to bubble pure O2 through the wort for up to half an hour, depending on the desired cell growth.

Once aerated, the wort is ready for healthy yeast (ideally at high krausen) to be pitched for fermentation. As the culture works through growth lag and towards respiratory metabolism, we have a few stress-free hours to reflect on the journey. From malted barley to sugar-rich wort, what began weeks earlier as field seeds have been carefully transformed by germination, kilning, milling, mashing, lautering, boiling, and cooling cycles. We stand now at the fulcrum between cooking and fermenting. The yeast takes over primary creative duties as we assume a support role to maintain conditions for clean fermentation towards the final glass.

Chapter 7

Brewing Equipment and Techniques for Beginners

The path to pouring your first perfect pint of homebrew starts with gathering your essential brewing tools. As you set up your kit and fill in the gaps over time, keep this maxim of the hobby in mind - there's always another piece of gear to add or upgrade. But you can get started on the fundamentals without breaking the bank or filling a barn. Here's the minimum to tap into this timeless craft of fermenting sugar water with your hands.

First up is the crown jewel of any brew rig: the brew kettle. This multipurpose vessel acts as your mash tun for steeping grains, your boil kettle for concentrating wort, and even a fermentation tank in a pinch. When selecting a stainless steel kettle, the cardinal rule is simple: go as big as your budget allows, up to around 15 gallons. Five- and six-gallon pots are standard starter sizes. At a minimum, aim for two gallons more capacity than your target batch size. The extra headroom prevents messy boilovers, gives you the flexibility to brew a range of beer styles, and futureproofs your system to scale up recipe sizes down the line. Kettles make do with essential features like volume markings and a sturdy welded handle. If you fall hard for homebrewing, you can upgrade to more advanced kettles with thermometer ports, ball valves, recirculation ports, and other bells and whistles. But for most beginners, a fundamental kettle is all you need to get cracking.

The following integral tool that makes the homebrew magic possible is your fermenter vessel, where you'll pitch your yeast. The standard option for beginners is an excellent old-fashioned six-gallon plastic bucket fermenter. Opt for a food-safe LDPE or PET plastic model featuring a tight-fitting screw-on lid with a rubber gasket and a smaller opening for your airlock. The deep, cylindrical shape and opaque plastic sides protect your brew from light exposure and give the yeast enough headspace to work their fermentation wonders. Some homebrew shops sell a bucket-and-lid pairing for around $15 to USD 20. If you like some added features, you can upgrade to buckets with extra ports for dry hopping or temperature probes, graduated volume markings, wider openings, rotating bases, and more. But even a barebones bucket has all you need to ferment five-gallon batches or split smaller volumes across multiple carboys.

The humble auto-siphon is a real backsaver moving onto necessary brew day accessories. As its name suggests, this magical device uses gravity and the power of physics to transfer liquid from your boil kettle to your fermenter or between vessels with zero effort. Gone are the days of risky pouring, straining, and painstaking ladling. You get smooth suction power on tap by pumping the siphon once or twice. Models with a built-in racking cane prevent sediment carryover as well. This tool quickly moves hot wort on brew day, kegging your finished beer or transferring batches for closed transfers. Most autosiphons cost between $10 to $25. Swing for the pricier stainless steel models to avoid plastic flavors leaching into your beers over time.

The humble stirring spoon is another all-star accessory for getting your DIY brewery up and running. Instead of using an everyday cooking spoon or spatula from your kitchen, getting dedicated brewing spoons for mashing in grains or whirlpooling hops is wise.

Food-grade plastic models like HDPE are more affordable and durable than wooden spoons that can rot over time. Look for large paddles or mash rakes with holes to improve liquid flow and penetration into mash grain beds. The oversized heads help mix big batches or break up dry spots in the mash tun. Be mindful when stirring a hot wort boil so you don't crack plastic spoons or burn your wooden models. Get two spoons to alternate for back-to-back brew days.

An inexpensive pH meter is a wise investment in monitoring and adjusting brewing water chemistry. The ability to measure mash pH and make small acid or salt additions can be the difference between a balanced beer that pops with flavor or a flat, hazy end product. You'll want to calibrate often with storage and cleaning solutions to keep your readings accurate. But even finicky cheap meters that need replacing yearly make a world of difference for the small upfront cost compared to sending out water reports. As your skills progress, you can upgrade to a more advanced pH meter with automatic temperature correction. But an entry-level model for around $30 to $40 bucks is adequate for most five-gallon extract batches from established recipes.

Moving the Malt from Grain to Glass

Despite common misconceptions, mashing does not involve stomping grains with your feet or beating them with a blunt object. On the contrary, the mashing process gently coaxes fermentable sugars out of malted grains using specific water temperatures. I liken it to steeping a giant pot of barley tea that will soon feed your future colony of busy yeast.

Mashing begins once your strike water and grains meet inside your mash tun vessel. For most five-gallon extract batches, a basic plastic cooler converted into a mash-lauter tun does the trick nicely. The thick insulation helps maintain temperatures throughout the 60 to 90-minute mash. As an optional doughing step, stir in a bit of your measured strike water first until the grain bed resembles a thick, sticky dough. This prevents dry clumps before introducing the bulk of your hot water.

Now comes the most tedious yet meditative phase of mashing - the saccharification rest. Maintain your mash in the ideal enzymatic temperature range of 148°F to 158°F. Here, malt enzymes break down starches into fermentable sugars. It is too low, under 148°F, and conversion slows to a crawl. It is too high, over 162°F, and you denature enzymes. I always tell new brewers to pick one target temperature, like 154°F, rather than fussing about raising the mash over multiple rests. Your palace of grain wants constancy.

Test often with a digital thermometer to avoid over or undershooting. Direct fire your brew kettle to heat water to raise mash temperatures in a pinch. Or sprinkle in near-boiling water if you overshoot upwards. Stir thoroughly after additions to distribute heat evenly. If your cooler mash tun isn't cutting it, upgrade to an electric brew-in-a-bag (BIAB) heating element system. Expensive, yes, but nothing beats automated temperature stability.

Now comes the moment of truth after an hour when iodine tincture confirms full saccharification. A couple of drops on a mash sample should show little to no dark purple. If black tones persist, stir and retest every 15 minutes until the purple fades. Don't worry - extra mash time won't hurt, provided you hold ideal temperature ranges. Enzymes sometimes need a nudge to chug along. Have faith in the process.

The Delicate Process of Lautering Wort

With starches converted fully into sugars, now you must separate the sweet liquid gold from soggy spent grains. Enter the subtle art of the lauter. Here, you'll witness the magical transformation of murky brown soupy mash into a clear, nutrition-filled wort destined for the fermenter.

Begin sparging by draining your mash tun through the false bottom into the awaiting kettle. Part art, part science, the goal is to rinse sugars from grains gently without compacting the delicate filter bed. Pour hot sparge water slowly over the grains in swirling circular motions. Think of yourself as a human sprinkler nozzle nurturing your grain bed. Care not to pour directly onto one area, channeling paths through compacted grains.

Pay attention to runoff clarity as you drain each batch of sweet wort. At first, expect muddy brown liquid as coarser grains slough through the filter bed. Then, the wort should flow darker amber but more apparent once the grain filter sets. Permanently halt the runoff stream if cloudiness persists to allow grains to resettle. Be patient and let filtration do its work correctly. Rushing this process risks a stuck mash, which takes much nuisance to unstick.

As sparging concludes, take pride in your giant kettle of hand-crafted sweet wort glowing a rich copper hue brimming with potential. But wait to discard those grains. First, Have fun running them through a strainer to collect that last half cup of sugary wort for a bonus. We homebrewers hate to waste resources- it's in our DNA encoded from those first Sumerian brewers!

Chapter 8

Designing Recipes and Beer Styles

Hops, malt, yeast, and water. These four simple ingredients are the foundation of every beer. But within that seemingly small ingredient list lurks incredible complexity and variation. Tiny tweaks to any of those four pillars can result in vastly different brews spanning dozens of distinctive beer styles. Learning the intricate differences between those styles gives a brewer immense creative freedom to design novel recipes and one-of-a-kind brews.

When designing a new recipe, the first step is selecting a style you wish to emulate while keeping in mind any personal preferences or twists you may want to add to make that brew your own. Let's walk through some of the significant beer-style families to outline their defining traits and get inspiration for potential recipes within each one.

Beginning brewers often start with approachable and easy-drinking pale ales or IPAs before venturing into darker, malt-forward stouts and porters. But regardless of where your taste preferences may start, understanding all prominent families provides context to tweak and sculpt recipes to match your vision. We'll progress from lighter-to-darker brews, discussing ingredients, techniques, and classic examples that exemplify the quintessential traits of each one.

First up on our tour is the pale ale family. Craft beer newcomers may associate the word "ale" with all beer, but ales are brewed differently from lagers, using distinct yeast strains and higher fermentation temperatures. American pale ales emerged from the craft beer boom in 1980s California, which pioneered the use of intensely floral and citrusy American hops. The same clean drinkability but bigger hop punch separates pale ales from their British cousins. Playing with different hop varieties and flameout/dry hop amounts allows recipe customization across the pale ale spectrum from mellow to aggressively bitter.

Traveling from California up the West Coast brings us to IPAs. India Pale Ales trace their origins even farther back to the British Empire shipping unfathomably hoppy beers to India. The critical distinction versus modern pale ales lies in higher gravity and IBUs from liberal hop dosing. That bitterness counterbalances thicker malt backbone and higher alcohol warming from additional base grains. They are imperializing an IPA by pushing to even greater extremes, results in tongue-numbing but intensely aromatic brews.

Coming back stateside while venturing into darker territory are brown and amber ales like nut browns or red IPAs. More specialty malts like Victory, chocolate, or caramel join pale base malts, with darker kilning contributing an array of toasted, nutty, or even faint chocolate flavors. Despite those sweet, bready malt aromas, judicious hopping maintains balance even with restrained bitterness. Experimenting with nutmeg, orange peel, or fall spice blends suits these malt-inclined but highly mixable beers.

We emerge from the amber-brown woodlands into the fierce highland territory of Scottish strong ales. The interplay of rich melanoidin-laden malts with the earthy, foraged botanical flavors of heather define Scottish styles like wee heavy and Scotch ale. Long boils caramelize wort sugars, forming that characteristic malt depth without needing specialty grains. Fermented cooler than English cousins, these beers let clean maltiness claim the spotlight, with hops staying politely in the background. Brewers can riff on the theme using local honey, fruit preserves, or other fermentable sugars true to the innovative spirit of hillside brochs and crofts that birthed this genre.

They are returning from Scotland and trekking south deposits us in Belgium, the ancestral holy land of eccentric beers. From abbey and Trappist styles, yeast proves to be as impactful on a recipe as malt and hops. Phenol and ester expressive strains like Chimay display their fruity, spicy terroir with flair. Sipping through the portfolio illustrates how tweakable wort composition interacts with those eccentric yeasts: tripels shine bright with massive, honeyed malt supporting summer apricot flavors. At the same time, dubbels instead offer molasses and dried fruit heft cut by licorice-like spice. Elsewhere, funky lambics and tart Flanders reds rely nearly entirely on wild microbes for acidity that complements oaky vintages blended for balance. With Belgian beers, designing a recipe means considering yeast and fermentation as prominent ingredients rather than afterthoughts.

Finally, capping off our world tour are the definitive malt bombs: stouts and porters. While often used interchangeably, porters originally referred to sweeter, lower gravity English beers compared to brawny, tar-black Irish dry stouts. Both styles depend heavily on roasted barley for defining burnt chocolate and espresso flavors, with variations dialing up adjuncts like oats for silky mouthfeel or lactose for milkshake creaminess. The darkest extreme lies in Russian imperial stouts packing intense cocoa with boozy heat perfect for aging in bourbon barrels or vanilla bean-spiked dessert renditions. Despite intimidating viscosity, no style offers more recipe improvisation for stout brewers to inject their personality into spotlight malt astringency balanced by just enough hops.

This whirlwind has underscored the breadth encapsulated by a seemingly simple list of ingredients. For brewers feeling overwhelmed facing that vast possibility, start by tasting diverse commercial examples and identifying flavors they enjoy. From there, reading about associated styles will connect those flavors to certain foundational grains, hops, yeasts, and techniques. Recipe formulation comes last after aligning personal preferences with concrete ingredients and methods to elicit your desired experience. Understanding ingredients grants the proficiency to formulate a style while deliberately deviating towards something new. That interplay underlies the craft itself.

Now that we've built shared language around significant beer families, we'll dive deeper into specific brewing ingredients and adjuncts to expand your repertoire for distorting and enhancing recipes with supplementary grains, herbs, barrels, and fermentable. So, let's prepare to get weird. Fruit purees, sea salt, 42-pound avocados, and more!

Armed with knowledge of significant beer styles, ingredients, and techniques, we can now shift focus toward actually formulating recipes. But a key question looms—where do you even start when facing the infinite possibilities of grain bills, hop additions, and yeast strains? Fear not the vastness! We will break down concrete steps that simplify recipe design from that overwhelming idea to holding your creation in hand.

First and foremost, deciding what beer style most appeals to your tastes. Are you craving crisp bitterness or warming bourbon sweetness? Do you want an easy-drinking refresher or a complex sipper? Reference earlier style breakdowns, remembering key traits, then find 1-2 commercial examples embodying qualities you hope to emulate. These become your blueprint for attributes to accentuate through recipe tweaks after.

Next, with desired characteristics in mind, compile relevant grains that can elicit those flavors using knowledge of how base and specialty malts influence wort. For instance, toasted bread and caramel in an amber ale may suggest pale malt supplemented by medium or dark crystal variants. Let your envisioned sensory experience guide malt selection, augmented by researched recipes of that style. Building ingredient familiarity eventually enables intuitive pairing by taste memory alone!

Having set a grain bill foundation for the intended malt flavor, the shift focuses upstream to prospective hop additions. Identify whether you want prominent bitterness or mostly flavor/aroma contributions, then target hop varieties are known for each. A West Coast IPA demands intense tropical fruitiness, for example, satisfied by later Citra/Mosaic doses. In contrast, a bohemian pilsner showcases spicy Saaz bittering, so first wort hopping works perfectly. Planning timing and locations for hop integration prevents muddling their Impact.

Now comes the most mystical pillar—yeast. While easily overlooked by beginners, yeast sculpts fermentation and the final beer profile arguably more than hops or grain. Consider their influence throughout recipe design, not as an afterthought. Estery English strains bootstrap desirable fruitiness in many ales but would overpower lagers requiring clean fermentation. Once again, let your aspirations guide selection, aided by manufacturer descriptions—finally, factor fermentation conditions like temperature that maintain yeast character.

These interwoven considerations ultimately synthesize your unique vision...on paper, at least. Finalizing a recipe still demands iteration through homebrew trials measuring results against imagination. Early attempts may surprise, given synergies between ingredients emerging mid-fermentation. Late citrus fade supersedes malt body, suggesting dialing back simplistic crystal malt tweaks. Stay receptive to each new brew unfolding past expectations, capturing learnings for the following great recipe waiting to shine through finer tuning!

Now a decade+ veteran homebrewer friend, Elliot, discovered immense value from an unexpected source that accelerated his iterative improvement process: competitions! Specifically, the National Homebrew Competition annually provides invaluable feedback from certified BJCP judges, strictly grading to style guide technicalities. The scoresheets return with detailed commentary on perceptible traits, whether positive standouts or flaws requiring adjustment. Implementing that qualitative advice catapults recipe refinement spanning months of solo tinkering into weeks by benefiting from generous outside expertise.

For illustration, when a hugely aromatic NEIPA of Elliot's scored surprisingly low on perceived hoppiness, the judge's notes revealed he needed to dry hop earlier at high krausen to magnify biotransformation effects. Tweaking that single timing for the next iteration amplified the hop punch fourfold! Now, he swears that entering every 4th brew objectively exposes improvement areas far better than relying on personal or friends' perceptions. External insights open our minds to facets easily overlooked internally. So, submit some samples to accelerate recipe design mastery through informed revision!

In closing, remember that an accurate homebrewer measures success not by perfectly matching commercial benchmarks but by how distinctly you share your artistic flair through ingredient choice and handling. Building proficiency by comprehending underlying beer chemistry transforms recipe formulation from a daunting mystery to a masterful creative outlet. But remember that even the seasoned experts continue tweaking and rediscovering across decades of experience. None among us unravel all the intricacies underlying each sip, nor should we! The beauty of this craft lies in lifelong incremental mastery, ever striving towards our changing ideal.

So stay bold with experiments, learn from failures, lean on friends' inputs, celebrate successes small and large, but above all...have fun! That homebrewer joy must never fade even as skills accumulate. Then you will look back amazed at early clumsy brews, proud at the progress made, yet eager for the subsequent great discovery over the horizon. And chances are high that very horizon keeps expanding wider the longer we chase it!

Now, then, enough hyperbolic reflections on the journey ahead. Let's ground back into practicalities on specific common brewing ingredients and adjuncts at homebrewers' disposal to act as finishing touches. First up, fruits...

Chapter 9

Common Brewing Ingredients and Adjuncts

Malting transforms cereal grains like barley into a brewing substrate rich in starches, sugars, proteins, and enzymes. Barley is the most common malted grain, but others like wheat, oats, corn, rice, and rye also serve essential roles. Unmalted grains lack the needed enzymes to convert their starches into fermentable sugars. That's where malting occurs - it activates enzymes and creates malt, nature's perfect sweet liquor to feed voracious yeast and make beer.

As a brewer, understand each grain's flavor, sugar potential, and protein levels. Barley malt conveys a clean, bready, biscuit taste. Wheat beers utilize more malted wheat, which lends a bready, doughy flavor. Corn lightens the body and adds alcohol without barley's flavor. 6-row barley has more enzymes than 2-row to handle adjunct grains. You decide what ratios help you achieve your recipe goals. Adjunct grains usually make up 15-30% of grist. Overuse adjuncts, and you lose flavor complexity. Underuse them; your beer may be a heavy, muddy mess lacking balance. As a novice brewer, stick with a simple pale ale grist of 80% 2-row barley malt and 20% wheat or flaked adjuncts. This opens creative doors while providing clean fermentability.

I learned the importance of base malts when developing an all-grain milk stout recipe. With lactose added, I used a grist of 75% 2-row, 15% flaked barley, 5% roasted barley, and 5% chocolate malt.

However, I accidentally bought roast wheat instead of flaked barley! My stout lacked body and head retention. The wheat lacked needed proteins. Another batch with barley flakes restored proper mouthfeel. A good base malt sets up a canvas. Specialty grains add accents.

The mashing process unlocks fermentable sugars and desirable flavors within malted grains. A mash temperature of around 150°F activates starch and protein-converting enzymes. This "liquefies" the grain bed into the sweet liquid brewers call wort. Pulling wort too soon under-converts starches, leaving hazy, sweet beer prone to infection. Let it rest too long, and it risks astringency. I recommend 60-90 minutes to ensure most starches convert while avoiding excess tannin extraction. Test your mash pH, too! The ideal range is 5.2-5.6. Add acid or alkaline salts as needed. Low mash pH promotes complete conversion and wort clarity. I once brewed with water far too alkaline. My beer was a cloudy, cloying mess until I took chemistry seriously!

Another tip - try stepping up the mash temperature for certain beers. Raise it to 160°F for the last 20 minutes when making solid ales. This ensures more unfermentable sugars remain, adding body and head retention. Or try a protein rest around 122°F to modify wheat beers prone to haze. Even lager brewing utilizes a 145°F fermentability rest followed by a 155°F conversion rest for their more straightforward, crisper profile. Each approach tailors its composition to style goals.

The journey from raw grain to glass begins at the malt house. Base malts deserve your attention as a brewer. Learn their unique attributes. Perfect your mash to maximize extraction. Sip the sweet words and appreciate Malt's foundational role. Blending various grains opens creative possibilities, but base malts build scaffolds to drape specialty ingredients. They tie each brew together into cohesive themes. Without them, you merely gather disconnected notes lacking harmony or structure. Raise a pint this weekend to celebrate humble malted barley - the source sustaining beer's endless march through history! Expanding Ingredient Horizons

As discussed earlier, the base malt builds a beer's foundations. Yet adjunct grains open creative doors by adding unique flavors or enhancing drinkability. They allow customization based on style goals or what ingredients are available. Let's survey some popular options.

Many novice brewers first utilize flaked maize as it lightens the body and boosts alcohol content. Produced by steam-rolling or flaking whole corn kernels after corn has been malted, it contributes a sweet, grainy flavor. Larger breweries add corn grits to their flagship lagers, but homebrew-scaled flakes offer similar fermentability and body-lightening. The key is balancing flaked maize such that it enhances drinkability without thinning the body excessively. I recommend 10-20% flakes in most styles in the total grain bill. One exception is cream ales. Their hallmark crispness comes from pushing maize up to 40% alongside pale malt.

Another easy addition is flaked wheat. Made similarly through steaming then rolling wheat kernels, it lends a bready, doughy flavor that accentuates a beer's maltiness. The proteins also boost head formation and retention. As little as 10-15% flaked wheat makes a beautiful difference in many ales. I recommend it in Belgian witbiers, where spice and citrus notes mingle with soft wheatiness. Or maximize wheat at 50%+ for authentic wheat beers like Hefeweizens showcasing cloves and bready esters. Gluten-free brewers have found sorghum, millet, or rice flakes help compensate for barley's absence.

Oatmeal intrigues through its silkiness. Around 10% in oatmeal stouts or brown ales to enhance body and mouthfeel. I also add modest amounts when brewing Scottish export ales for smooth, lusciousness-supporting caramel malt flavors. Groats or rolled oats work best as their flattened shape exposes more starch for conversion. Remember that excess oatmeal risks a stuck sparge during lautering or wort separation. Be prepared to vorlauf slowly when utilizing oatmeal to avoid a gluey mash mess!

Rye continues gaining popularity for its spicy, earthy kick to various beer styles. Its huskless nature makes using more than 20% in a grist difficult, but even small amounts make their presence known. The sharply aromatic quality balances malt sweetness beautifully. Rye porters, pale ales, or saisons make excellent showcases. I particularly love its marriage with citrus hops. Experiment with different forms, too. Malted rye sharpens the spice, but flaked or torrified rye softens it toward doughiness. Toasted rye amps the intensity further.

Do not overlook simple sugar additions, either. Brewers utilize inverted sugar syrup, dextrose, or plain table sugar to thin the body, boost abv, or dry out finishes. Belgian golden solid ales often get 10-15% sugar for effervescent drinkability. For comparison, an English barleywine might only use 5% sugar to avoid overwhelming malt complexity. And certain fruit-forward American wild ales push modest sugar levels to 20%+ alongside fruit purees. The possibilities abound!

Finally, remember that non-barley alternatives lack certain enzymes or protein levels compared to malted barley. Use barley malt extract or add 6-row into the grist if using over 20% alternative grains. Their surplus enzymes help ensure starch conversion. Or try cereal mashing flakes in warm water to gelatinize starches before adding the mash. Wort clarity and fermentability will thank you.

I encourage embracing these adjuncts to put your stamp on recipes! Blend different grains based on available ingredients and the flavors you wish to highlight. Brew the same base recipe with alternating additions until each one's imprint is understood. There is no rigid formula. Adjunct experimentation helps move us beyond assumed constraints toward richer beer diversity. Trust your palate's guidance through sensory exploration. Allow new grains to broaden perspective just as travel reshapes worldviews. Then, watch your imagination transform an everyday pint into your liquid canvas for artistic expression!

Chapter 10

Managing Fermentation Temperature and Health

Ah yes, fermentation - that bubbling, buzzing, magical process that turns sugary wort into delicious, alcoholic beer. Getting fermentation right is critical; managing temperature is at the heart of fermentation success. New brewers often need to pay more attention to temperature control. Still, veterans know that nothing determines the final character of a beer more than what happens during primary and secondary fermentation.

I made this mistake early on. Eager to get brewing, I tossed together my first few beers without any accurate temperature regulation or monitoring beyond sticking a thermometer on the side of the fermenter. My apartment was often hot and cold at seemingly random intervals. As you can imagine, the beer turned out all over the place - some drinkable if dull, others with solid off-flavors. I scratched, wondering what went wrong until a wise old homebrew shop owner asked about my fermentation temperatures. The light bulb went on, and I realized no recipe tweaking would fix what happened after the boil.

Proper temperature control lets you pinpoint the exact environment best suited for your yeast. Each strain has an ideal range that unlocks the necessary biological reactions to yield great flavors, adequate alcohol, and healthy fermentation. Monitoring the temperature also prevents sticking points, allowing you to take corrective action before problems arise. Wide swings introduce many issues - you risk stressed yeast, incomplete fermentation, strange esters, fuse alcohols, excess sulfur, and more. I once had a Belgian Strong Ale held at 85°F for the first three days of fermentation due to a hot spell. It was undrinkable - all bubblegum and green apple with a harsh burn.

In this chapter, we'll cover the fundamentals of managing temperature during fermentation: understanding yeast requirements, options for monitoring and regulating temperature, hitting optimal ranges for everyday styles, and troubleshooting issues when they emerge. Master these techniques, and you'll find greater consistency, happier yeast, and significant improvements in your homebrew.

Monitoring and Controlling Fermentation Temperature

The foundation of temperature control lies in vigilant monitoring. Observing and recording temperatures allows you to spot problems early and make adjustments. Luckily, keeping tabs on your fermentation is straightforward with the right gear. Let's run through some monitoring fundamentals.

First and foremost, invest in a good thermometer. Digital probe thermometers that continuously display current temperature work fantastically. Place the probe against the side or top of the fermenter, securing it with tape, bloggers, or insulation to ensure good surface contact. Take initial readings every 12 hours, tracking the temperature swings. Pay special attention during the first 72 hours when the most active fermentation occurs. Temperatures often peak on days 2-4.

Make observations during this stretch. Is it sticking to the yeast's ideal range? Does it align historically with the same recipe? Did you recently replace a heating pad or add a new temperature control system that could impact readings? Significant deviations merit investigation and potentially adjusting your temperature regulation approach to compensate. But within expected fluctuations? Carry on and have another homebrew!

Besides physically checking, WiFi-enabled or Bluetooth thermometers now allow remote temperature tracking through smartphone apps and online dashboards. No more trekking down to the basement to read a thermometer! My geeky side loves data, so I outfitted all my fermentation vessels with wireless sensors feeding readings to my BrewMonitor portal. One glance, 8and I know precisely what is happening across all batches. I was highly recommended for the obsessive temperature watcher.

So you've begun monitoring - excellent first step! But observation alone means nothing unless you plan to act—time to cover regulating and controlling temperature during fermentation. Lucky for us homebrewers, many options fit any budget and setup. We'll tackle those next.

Regulating Fermentation Temperature

As homebrewers, we must work with the environmental conditions available to us. For most, this involves finding ways to heat actively or excellent fermenting beer rather than relying on ambient temperatures alone. Thankfully, both heating and cooling options abound for reasonable prices these days. Let's explore some of the most common temperature regulation strategies.

One of the simplest and most cost-effective heating methods involves wrapping the fermenter with a pad or belt. Heating pads come in electric and USB-powered models, providing sustained low heat that is perfect for maintaining temperatures. I use a brew belt wrapped around my stainless fermenters with great success. Set to 72°F, it keeps the beer at 66°F ambient, perfect for most ales. Just monitor closely and adjust the belt intensity to avoid overheating.

For more precise heating capabilities, a temperature controller paired with a heat source allows the customization of ramps and thresholds. Controllers have probe inputs to track beer temperature directly rather than ambient air or the surface of the heating device. I use an Inkbird with a heat wrap plugged into the power outlet, with the power cutting on and off based on my programmed temperature thresholds. This automated regulation reduces checking while still keeping the beer within tight bounds. Models from Johnson Controls and Brewjacket work similarly.

Turning to cool options, the most straightforward approach involves finding a suitably cold area to ferment, like a basement or garage. My friend ops to ferment lagers and hybrids year-round in his finished basement, holding steady at 55°F. No special equipment is needed! For those without access to chilly real estate, purpose-built cooling chambers offer an affordable alternative to chest freezers. Cooler-style chambers from FermWrap, Brew Hauler, and Keg King regulate down to larger temperatures with compressor units similar to a mini-fridge. Just slide your fermenter in and set the target temp.

As the premium solution, converting a chest freezer or mini-fridge into a fermentation chamber grants exact temperature control. The conversion process isn't overly complex - drill a hole for probe wires, add a temperature controller to turn the freezer on and off, and voila! I use an old freezer with an STC-1000 controller, and regular carboy handles to lift fermenters in and out. Dialed into my Hefeweizen profile, I get beautiful, consistent ferments. The only downside lies in higher equipment costs compared to the other solutions.

In reality, all temperature regulation is balancing precision against budget and complexity. Thankfully, this spectrum means homebrewers have many options to fit their needs. I employ different solutions across my setup, from the simple brew belt for ales to the converted freezer for lagers and hybrids. I encourage brewers to start simply and upgrade as their experience and batch sizes expand.

Preventing Contamination and Off-Flavors

Besides hitting target fermentation temperatures, monitoring serves another critical purpose - spotting early signs of contamination or off-flavor development before batches are thoroughly spoiled. Nothing hurts more than dumping 20 gallons of rancid beer! Prevention will always be more accessible than salvaging gone-wrong fermentations. Heeding a few simple "rules of thumb" goes a long way toward avoiding disasters:

- Strange odor - Trouble likely brews if you detect abnormal or off-putting scents like sulfur, nail polish remover, or rotten eggs. Infections often produce telltale smells identifiable to experienced palates. But when in doubt, trust your nose - funky is never good this early.

- Visual irregularities - Look closely at the beer and yeast layers. Be concerned if colors seem dull or oddly hued rather than bright, bubbly white yeast. Likewise, over-active fermentation with blowing-out airlocks or extremely thick krausen may indicate contamination from wild yeast or bacteria.

- Stalling activity - No visible fermentation activity for over 48 hours, especially with gravities above expected final ranges. Be worried. Healthy, viable yeasts working on available sugars rarely go that long without bubbles or other signs of life.

Catching issues early allows for troubleshooting and recovery tactics: raising temperatures to encourage yeast activity, repitching fresh, healthy yeast, or carefully racking under CO2 into a purged secondary vessel. Dramatic flavor defects, however, may warrant disposal and a deep cleaning of all equipment. Trust all your senses, leverage your records to compare against previous batches, and never hesitate to ask other brewers when uncertain. An extra set of experienced eyes can spot problems you may overlook. With vigilance and decisiveness, maintaining fermentation health becomes that much easier.

In closing, embrace temperature monitoring and control as critical to crafting clean, consistent homebrewed beer. Understanding yeast strain characteristics, employing measurement best practices, regulating optimal temperature ranges, and staying alert to contamination risks combine to make all the difference between good beer and undrinkable swill. My early inconsistent batches taught me such lessons firsthand. Years later, with a bank of controls and recording, I achieve great results brew after brew. Follow these lessons yourself, be patient, dial in processes, and your tastebuds will thank you!

Hops, Malt, Yeast, and Water

Chapter 11

Clarifying, Carbonating, Packaging, and Cellaring

A critical step before packaging your freshly brewed beer is clarifying it by removing excess proteins, hop residues, and yeast in suspension. This helps produce a more precise final product with improved shelf stability and aesthetic appeal. As homebrewers, we have a few approaches to clarify beer naturally over time or speed up the process with fining agents.

Cold crashing is a popular method that relies on temperature rather than additions. About two days before packaging, simply place your fermentation vessel in a cold refrigerator, basement, or snowbank at temperatures between 32-45 degrees Fahrenheit for 1-2 days. The sudden hard shocks the yeast, causing the remaining cells in suspension to flocculate or clump together and settle out to the bottom. This removes significant yeast and proteins over time, but be wary of temperatures dipping too low and inadvertently freezing or over-chilling the beer. Consider transferring to a secondary vessel beforehand to ease fermentation temperature control.

Gelatin fining is another common technique that acts through charge interactions. By dissolving unflavored gelatin powder in hot water and stirring it into the fantastic fermented beer, the gelatin molecules bind to positively charged proteins. These form large complexes that rapidly sink, pulling out haze-causing compounds. Only a tiny half teaspoon is needed for five gallons. Gelatin must make complete contact, so avoid dumping powder directly on the beer's surface. Give at least two days of contact time before bottling.

Irish moss and whirl floc tablets contain carrageenan, a negatively charged algae derivative that grabs positively charged proteins through the exact mechanism. These aids are added to the brew kettle during the boil stage's last 10-15 minutes. The earlier addition allows the carrageenan complexes sufficient time to bind protein fragments from malt and hops, settling into the trub instead of staying suspended post-fermentation.

Isinglass finings originate from the dried swim bladders of fish like sturgeon. The collagen strands make excellent settling agents to clarify wine and beer by attracting yeast cells and interacting with haze proteins. Homebrew supply stores offer it as transparent sheets that must be soaked and dissolved into water before mixing into beer. For vegetarian brewers, Fine Clear is a vegan-friendly substitute made of silicate dioxide. It works similarly but without animal products.

Once fined or cold-crashed, allow beers to remain untouched for at least two days for visible clearing effects. Elevating fermenters onto higher surfaces quickens the downward precipitation process. Still, beers shed more sediment than high-carbonation styles, but all benefit from greater clarity. Visually inspect samples drawn from the mid-level or siphon spigot to confirm brightening. Removing from the very top or bottom could mislead on actual appearance. Patience is vital as rushivitalthis process risks losing sediment back into suspension when moving to packaging.

After a week or longer untouched, homebrew may appear clear yet retain microscopic particulate unless carefully siphoned or racked into a bottling bucket or keg. I recommend pulling equipment to gently transfer clear beer away from the compacted trub pile using flexible tubing, leaving anything settled behind. If directly bottling from a carboy is unavoidable, simply watch the siphon inlet closely, stopping transfer before the intake touches settled sediment. This avoids picking excess backup. Have a flashlight handy to peer inside carboys, stopping when yeast is visible accumulating near the tube opening.

While swimming particles may reappear after initially clarifying, the beer's appearance only improves. Yeast and proteins continue bonding together and dropping out for months post-packaging. Homebrewers notice the difference between sampling early bottles versus well-conditioned and aged ones. So do not worry if beers are initially hazy pre-carbonation. Providing sufficient settling time and avoiding heavy particulate carrying over into packages allows our beloved elixir to brighten beautifully in time. Cheers to clearer brews!

The Bubbly Blessing: Carbonating Homebrew

Though flat beer remains an entertaining conversation at parties, we truly desire that lively carbonation to lift aromas and please the palate. Adding CO_2 creates refreshing effervescence, a creamy, frothy head, and lively bubbles dancing playfully through the glass. But properly carbonating our lovingly crafted brews requires precise technique to avoid foamy fiascos exploding on kitchen ceilings.

After allowing green beer to condition post-fermentation, whether naturally settling or clarifying through fining methods as previously discussed, the next vital phase commences - safely infusing carbonation. While forcing CO_2 into solution under pressure works fine for commercial operations, most homebrewers rely on bottle conditioning using residual yeast. Much like initial fermentation, the remaining viable cells metabolize small amounts of priming sugar introduced evenly into the batch before sealing into bottles. As the yeast consumes and transforms this dose of carbohydrates into CO2 and a trace of alcohol, volumes of gas are generated and trapped within the bottles to carbonate naturally over time.

Correcting the priming dosage proves critical, as both under and over-carbonation spoil the drinking experience. Target a ratio of 2.0-2.5 volumes of CO2 depending on the beer style, referring to volumes of gas measured at standard temperature and pressure compared to the liquid volume. At 70°F, every gram of corn sugar or DME added per liter of beer contributes 0.5 volumes of carbonation. For less math, use online priming calculators to enter specifics. Once determined, thoroughly boil and cool this precise measure with water into an inverted sugar solution before evenly distributing it into the full batch stotalto ensure an equal dose per bottle.

After careful sugar infusion, siphoning into bottles must leave behind as much sediment as possible to avoid further yeast activity skewing carbonation. Any residual particulate will consume additional sugar unevenly. I highly advise a clarifying cold-crash and using a bottling bucket with a siphon setup to geensurer obvious beer. Before sealing, make sure bottles are carefully cleaned, sanitized, and free of surface dust and oi handling to prevent contamination issues. Then, finally, cap each bottle tightly—store for a minimum of 2 weeks, around 64-75°F, to develop carbonation. Chill one sacrificial bottle every few days to test pressure building through the crown cap and sample flavor until reaching the preferred bubbly level. If concerned about over-carbonating or explosions from possible infections, burp the other bottles occasionally. Seek that magical Goldilocks balance!

Packaging Up the Beer

While most novice brewers begin bottling their beloved nectar, many upgrade to corny kegs for easier handling and better preservation. These small five-gallon soda kegs seal oxygen far longer than caps and bottles over months. They connect directly to taps instead of requiring individual opening. Although kegging demands some equipment investment into cylinders, regulators, and seals, it avoids hours of tedious bottling sessions and provides better long-term storage.

If sticking to bottling, choose thicker hybrid bottles over cheap light variants to prevent breakage and UV damage. Soak used commercial bottles overnight in Oxyclean to lift labels and sterilize. New bottles just need a quick sanitizing before that first use. Lever-capped flip-top growlers make an excellent large-format bottle option as well. When handling and storing, be highly conscious of limiting oxygen intake. Top-up bottles to within an inch of the neck, leaving minimal headspace for air. Cap securely on foam if detectable. And avoid splashing transfers that whisk in oxygen. Anaerobic conditions preserve freshness. Please use no questionable methods like adding marbles or water to displace headspace as these ruin the drinking experience.

Cellaring Homebrew Gracefully

Under optimal cooler conditions between 50-60°F and out of sunlight, many styles retain peak flavor for three months or longer before fading. Standard bottles assist with short-term aging up to six months. Beyond that duration, strong beers warrant repitching with champagne yeast under cork and cage to condition further. When cellaring for over a year, ensure absolute sterile conditions to avoid the devastating heartbreak of cracking open that special occasion bottle only to find it has soured or spoiled drinkable.

For long-term aging exceeding multiple years, higher alcohol imperial styles and wild fermentations deserve upgrading into thick-walled 750ml wine bottles capped with Belgium cork and wire baskets. These tolerate many years cellared vertically to keep the corks moistened. Monitor yearly at a minimum by temporarily uprighting to check fill level and cork integrity. Top up any ullage lost to evaporation with a sterile brew to restore liquid height to the bottle's neck. Also, sample occasionally over the aging timeline to determine if further aging improves complexity or if the beer peaks and starts declining. Drain pours are better learning experiences than unexpected disappointments years later!

In conclusion, while fermentation sews together that tasty liquid bread, additional steps preparing our beers for optimal presentation let them shine at their best for current enjoyment or future celebrations. So be sure to give your brews the proper send-off through an attentive series of transfers, precision carbonation, intelligent packaging, and grace over time. Now, let us revel in the fruits of our patience paired with good company!

Chapter 12

Basic Homebrewing Mistakes and How to Avoid Them

Sanitation Seems Like a Drag, But Sloppy Practices Spell Disaster

Becoming obsessed with perfectly scrubbing every last inch of our equipment hardly screams "fun hobby" at first glance. However, ensuring proper sanitation is paramount behind fermentation in crafting crisp, clean homebrew. Even minute traces of wild yeast or infectious bacteria rapidly propagating across sugary worts resemble a prison breakout with0500 convicts storming the countryside. What initially seems like overkill and excessive scrubbing prevents our beloved brew from becoming a bubbly science experiment nobody dares sample twice.

As a novice homebrewer many years ago, I laughed off stern warnings from seasoned veterans regarding sanitation. Full of youthful optimism and confidence bordering on hubris, I hardly thought leaving a few pieces of equipment drying overnight could ruin an entire batch. Oh, how wrong I was. That fateful batch transformed my naïve nonchalance into becoming a sanitation zealot.

That experience taught me proper sanitation does not simply enhance your final beer; it makes or breaks it. Much like constructing a pristine sandcastle at the beach, building up our scrumptious beer requires careful effort, but only one misstep will come crashing down. Thankfully, once sanitation's importance clicks, maintaining these new habits becomes second nature. Let's explore proper techniques so you avoid my same hard lesson. This chapter covers common sanitation mistakes new homebrewers make and how to dodge these pitfalls.

Rushing Equipment Cleanup and Forgetting the Smaller Pieces

Whether exhausted from a long brew day or anxiously awaiting tasting the final product, skipping proper post-boil equipment cleaning seems tempting. Especially with complicated systems involving pumps, plates, chillers, and various hoses, thoroughly breaking down and scrubbing every inch appears daunting. The hot side holding wort remains highly vulnerable to contamination and forgetting just one small piece provides plenty of surface area for bacteria to sneak in.

I confess more than once, I left tubes, quick disconnects, and pumps simply soaking in water overnight before fully sanitizing them the next day. My impatience quickly spawned complications, though. One time, in particular, my neglected pump pickup tube and the chill plate incubated a biofilm that infected my next batch with a bitter metallic flavor. It required entirely replacing several pieces to eliminate the stubborn colony that kept repopulating. Now I mandate a strict post-boil breakdown checklist after each brew session to avoid missing any spots. I also prepare spare pumps, tubing, o-rings, and gaskets in case I discover hidden grime.

Getting Overwhelmed with Turbo Sanitizer Solutions but Forgetting Proper Contact Time

New homebrewers anxious to follow best practices often mix their sanitizer to almost dangerous concentrations. However, only some realize contact time stands equally vital as sanitizer strength. Dunking equipment in even the strongest iodophor or acid blend for only 30 seconds resembles quickly dipping your hands in hot wax and then peeling it right back off. At best, you achieve limited surface level cleaning. More often, you simply spread contaminants around while dangerously handling corrosive chemicals.

Recently, a buddy of mine, Eric, nearly sent himself to urgent care by obsessively trying to eliminate an imaginary infection plaguing his batches. He brewed his everyday recipe four times in a row, subtly tweaking procedures to dial in the flavor. Each successive batch came out slightly from his last best effort, though. Upping his sanitizer to triple strength and soaking gear for hours on end, his frustration peaked when his fourth attempt tasted more sour.

As the unofficial infection advisor among my homebrew friends, he pleaded for my wisdom after his ever-more-stringent efforts continued to fail. I asked him to walk me through his process and felt confident ruling out sanitization as the culprit. Only while helping him lift a carboy to dump a batch did I notice his forearms beet red and beginning to blister. Still not wearing gloves while practically bathing in acid for hours, I finally caught up to him. His next batch came out perfectly clean after properly balancing sanitizer concentration and contact time while wearing gloves. So remember, strongly sanitizing for 30 seconds fails compared to properly sanitizing for 2 minutes.

Getting Lazy About Star San Foam and Misunderstanding No Rinse

Given Star San's phenomenal capabilities, many homebrewers simply associate its vibrant foam with "sanitized goodness" and leave covered equipment sitting for long durations before use. Additionally, the "no rinse" phrasing tricks some brewers into skipping post-sanitization spray downs. However, that thick foam itself does not adequately sanitize, and allowing it to dry sacrifices sanitization. Star San requires actively swishing contact for full potency and works by chemically altering cell wall structures. Once its foamy barrier evaporates and dries, it loses this capability.

My friend Chris learned this lesson when he took the no-rinse label too literally. An early extract brewer at the time, he thoroughly sprayed down his plastic fermenter and let it drip dry for over an hour pre-boil as he gathered other supplies. In his mind, the initial foam release ensured peak sanitation and the no rinse aspect meant skipping any spraying afterward. However, returning to discover caked dry residue and not rinsing meant active microbes quickly hitched a ride into his wort. A week later, his airlock bubbled away as normal but revealed a phenolic batch upon tasting. Since then, he sprays Star San foam across all surfaces but immediately rinses afterward with clean, sterile water.

So, in summary, vibrant foam signals a freshly active solution but requires swishing contact, not just passive soaking. Also, always spray a water rinse afterwards, regardless of no rinse claims. Properly balancing timing, concentration levels, application methods, and contact ultimately determine success.

Attempting to Sanitize Visibly Dirty, Greasy or Moldy Equipment

Whether faced with old mildewy gear rescued from basements, inheriting questionable equipment from others, or dealing with grimy kettles and disgustingly clogged lines mid-brew, attempting to sanitize dirty equipment typically fails. At best, you waste good chemicals and at worst, make contamination issues much worse. Just like refusing to clean visible stains off dishes before running them through the dishwasher, set in organic matter prevents sanitizers from adequately penetrating cracked grain husks, grease, or grime.

A scary experience from my early all-grain days taught me that lesson vividly. Eager to expand my 5-gallon extract brewing into larger 10-gallon all-grain batches, I scored a good deal on a used mash tun missing only the false bottom. Or so I believed upon first inspection. The previous owner performed zero cleaning on some hidden inner crevices before storing it away a final time. Hoisting the awkward cylindrical cooler to tilt and scrape every last bit of old grain debris and solidified hop sludge pushed my patience and disgust tolerance to their very limits.

However, once I finished removing actual pounds of compacted slime, I ignorantly assumed tossing in my hottest PBW mix for an hour succeeded in thoroughly preparing the tun for brewing. Still oblivious following sanitizing afterward, I mashed in my standard pale ale recipe as usual. Only when vorlaufing my first runnings did I discover the horrors I unleashed? Floating bits of grey muck comingled with the sweet wort indeed indicated leftover debris deep in etched scratches, still escaping my cleaning efforts somehow. Sadly, I had to dump the entire batch and fully dismantle the mash tun to address chambers and gaps I couldn't reach before. Now, I always check secondhand gear under bright light from every angle before even contemplating brewing with it.

In closing, sanitizing fails as an adequate replacement for cleaning. Ensure all equipment shines as clean as new before even attempting our vital last sanitization step. Sometimes, this requires fully disassembling intricate systems and soaking specific attachments individually by hand if mechanical cleaning cannot scour every surface. Future, you will thank present for taking the time and effort up front, rather than realizing too late that quick fixes do more harm than good. Proper sequencing of thoroughly cleaning and then fully sanitizing remains critical to success.

Covering these common sanitation mistakes helps you internalize best practices as second nature. Sanitation certainly involves some tedious aspects, but preventing ruined beer makes the effort worthwhile. Next, we will explore common fermentation errors and how to avoid them. Once you dial in strong sanitation habits, maintaining healthy, active fermentation is our second biggest priority!

When Fermentation Turns Funky: Identifying Infection Culprits

As homebrewers, we lovingly nurture our worts through brewing in hopes of a smooth fermentation yielding scrumptious finished beer. However, just as unpredictable variables affect human health, rogue microbes or unstable conditions can also stress our fermenting beer. Before advising prevention methods, correctly identifying the type of infection proves critical.

Attempting to remedy a situation without understanding its root cause typically exacerbates issues. Unfortunately, too many well-intentioned homebrewers jump the gun trying advanced techniques to "save" batches. While advanced troubleshooting helps manage healthy fermentations, misdiagnosing sick batches as infection-free leads brewers astray.

My friend Steve recently fell into this trap when he incorrectly assumed his latest malty stout needed more aging time. Loath to dump five gallons of enveloping goodness, he racked the beer twice, trying to clear up the persisting haziness. However, the beer maintained a cloying sweetness for months longer than expected. I regret not sampling this batch before first hearing about the stalled fermentation. One whiff instantly transported me into tropical fruit juice territory far from roasty decadence. Steve's batch suffered from a lactobacillus infection, not just plate-chilling haze requiring patience.

6

When we identified the actual issue, he handled the equipment and bottles multiple times while racking under false assumptions. This spread the contamination into adjoining areas of his brewery, setting up even more significant issues down the road. Now we know to verify infections early before attempting any remedy, lest we spiral out of control. Let's explore common beer illnesses appearing during fermentation and how to spot them.

Watching the Clock to Notice Stalled Fermentations

Nothing immediately signals looming problems like our trusty airlock suddenly showing minimal bubbling activity during peak fermentation. While various explanations exist for reduced airlock activity, assuming your sanitation held strong, yeast health issues probably play some role. However, different strains showcase varying vigor and flocculation levels anyway. Monitoring the clock provides more reliable metrics.

I advise noting your batch's first visible activity once introduced into the fermenter. Depending on pitch rate and other factors, 12-36 hours typically pass before observing the first tiny bubbles. If using an active starter around high krausen, fermentation kicks off sometimes in under 8 hours. However long it takes your specific wort to show initial movement, begin timing from that point forward. Start checking gravity once 60-70% of your yeast's typical attenuation range passes without hitting the final gravity.

For example, if you pitch an English ale strain with 75% average attenuation into 1.055 wort, begin evaluating if terminal gravity fails to drop around 10 gravity points lower by day 4 (60% of typical 16 point attenuation). If gravity ceases changing after only 10-12 points, stuck fermentation issues likely play a role. Act quickly to differentiate between remaining sugars due to wort composition factors or yeast problems.

Inspecting Krausen and Yeast Cake Formations

The actual appearance and activity of the krausen during peak fermentation reveal much about your beer's health. I advise checking your fermenter daily whenever possible during those first critical days post-pitching. Look for visible tiny bubbles streaming upward through the rich, creamy foam topping your fermenting beer. Observe the color and texture, too – crisp white bubbles signal happy yeast, while odd colors or sliminess indicate bacteria.

Chapter 13

Tasting Beer: Developing Your Palate

The Complex World of Beer Flavors

As you progress into craft beer, you'll find an incredibly diverse and complex world of flavors and aromas to discover. Far beyond just "bitter" or "malty," the tastes and smells of beer draw from a broad spectrum of foods, spices, flowers, fruits, and more. Developing your "beer palate" is one of the most rewarding parts of becoming an enthusiast.

The Source of Flavors in Beer

Where do all these flavors come from? Primarily, the richness comes from the interplay of the four main ingredients: malt, hops, yeast, and water. Malted barley lends sweet, bready, toasty, and nutty flavors. Hops provide balancing bitterness plus fruity, herbal, floral, and earthy qualities depending on the variety. Yeast drives the fermentation that converts sugars into alcohol and carbon dioxide, leaving subtle " yeasty" esters and phenols behind. Even water chemistry plays a role, with minerals accentuating malt, hop, or yeast attributes. Many brewers also creatively use adjuncts, from fruits to spices to coffee and more. Masterful brewers combine these elements into harmonious concoctions bursting with aroma and taste.

Developing Your Palate

Labeling flavors takes time and experience because our palates must be trained. We have around 10,000 taste buds on our tongue, soft palate, and upper throat. These connect to our olfactory system through the nasal passage to perceive aromas as we eat and drink. It takes conscious effort to awaken our senses. As wine tasters swirl and sniff to coax subtle notes from a glass, we must pay close attention as we sip and savor beer. Eventually,pickingk out key characteristic becomes second natures. Keeping detailed tasting notes trains both the mind and senses.

The "Flavor Wheel"

An invaluable tool is the beer flavor wheel. Professor Emeritus Charlie Bamforth of UC Davis crafted one of the originals while delving into the science behind brewing. It organizes descriptors into basic taste categories: sweet, sour, salty, bitter, and umami. From there, branches lead out to associated aromas. For example, malty sweetness connects to red apple, caramel, biscuit, and more in one direction, while bitter tannins link black tea and espresso in another. The wheel shows how flavors connect and where to search in each sip. There are many variations created by brewers and experts today.

The Importance of Objective Tasting

A key to improving is being as objective as possible, not just looking for what we expect or like. It requires focus, especially with bold or unfamiliar flavors. What may seem sharply bitter at first becomes detected as resinous, piney, or citric over time. Some flavors only emerge as beer warms slightly from fridge temperatures. Others that were muted suddenly appear. Setting aside preconceptions allows subtleties to come forward over several careful sips. If descriptors still don't fit, make up your colorful words!

Building Your Beer Flavor Library

Compiling detailed notes for the growing list of beers you try provides learning material. After a while, patterns emerge - you associate certain flavors with ingredients, brewing processes, or beer styles. You build a "flavor library" in your mind. Connecting experiences is how we make sense of new stimuli. When tasting a beer for the first time, your brain searches for connections to similar taste memories, dredging up descriptors. With conscious repetition, identifying characteristics becomes natural.

Erasing Taste Buds Between Samples

When tasting sevonal beers in a flight, a palate cleanser helps erase leftover flavors clinging to taste buds so each one can be evaluated on its own accurate merits. Water or very bland crackers do the trick, but unsweetened dark chocolate, pretzels or apple slices work well too. Believe it or not, the best practice might come from commercial coffee cuppers. They slurp a spoonful, swish it forcefully around their whole mouth, then spit it out! This coats every inch of the palate to pull oils and residue from all surfaces. For beer though, a good swish of water or nibble of cracker typically suffices!

The Six Basic Tastes

Let's explore how to recognize the fundamentals - sweet, sour, salty, bitter, umami and alcohol. Grasping these helps anchor more complex aromas. They form the framework everything else hangs on. We'll dive deeper into full categories like malt, hop,s and fermentation characteristic shortlys. For now, focus on dialing each of these simple tastes into your sensory toolbox.

- Sweet - The backbone malt bill lends sweetness in balance to bitterness from hops. Associated flavors of honey, caramel, toffee, chocolate or bread can emerge depending on malt variety and kilning method. Does sweetness taste cloying, rich, delicate?
- Sour - In some beer styles, controlled addition of lactic acid bacteria purposefully sours the beer, lending puckering tartness akin to lemon, vinegar or yogurt. However, beware unintended infection by wild yeast or bacteria - acetic sourness signals a flawed beer. When appropriate though, does sourness seem smooth, creamy, sharp?
- Salty - Though unusual, some experimenters add a touch of salt to accentuate overall flavors. More indirectly, saline quality may suggest minerals from brewing water. Does salt seem out of balance or enhance other tastes?
- Bitter - Hops are the primary source of pleasurable bitterness to balance malt sweetness, adding an edge that keeps beers drinkable. They also contribute grassy, pine, citrus and floral notes. Does bitterness seem harsh, dense, smooth or delicate?
- Umami - This savory fifth taste often describes meaty richness. Umami in beer likely comes from amino acids reacting over time with compounds from malt and yeast. Roasted malts and higher alcohol beers more often show umami qualities, which may be earthy, brothy, or mouthwatering.
- Alcohol - Its warming presence ranges vastly depending on strength, from nearly invisible lacing to fierce heat. Does booziness overwhelm other flavors or blend harmoniously?

With attentive focus while tasting, pick apart where each primary flavor makes itself known. Note aromas attached to sweet maltiness apart from those clinging to bitter hops. Mark whether alcohol fights for attention or simmers quietly in the background. Compare how sourness differs from beer to beer. Pinpoint where an unexpected dash of saltiness peeks through. Train your brain to break apart and label basic elements automatically. This builds a solid sensory foundation onto which more intricate tastes overlay.

Malt Flavor & Aroma

The rich language around malt development deserves special mention. Hundreds of aroma and flavor compounds are created or enhanced by gently roasting the malted barley. As with coffee beans and cocoa nibs, applying low, steady heat via drying or kilning causes sugars and amino acids called melanoidins to caramelize. Even before roasting, malts exhibit grainy, doughy qualities from the base starch. The degree of roasting progresses through bread and cookie on toward toasted nuts, deep caramel, and finally bittersweet chocolate or espresso.

Pull apart these this malt characteristics beerer. How does malt express itself throughout the journey from crackery and bready paleness to toffee amber hues onto molasses or prune darkness? Detect nuttiness in the midst of roasty black malt. Take time exploring flavor libraries so you learn to spotlight subtle differences between biscuit versus bread crust versus graham cracker.

Further Malt Complexity

Actual grains introduced during or after brewing also provide distinctive malt aromas. Roasted barley isn't truly malted, so it skips the gentle germination stage, going straight to roasting instead. This adds a unique coffee and dark chocolate personality. Crystal or cara malts get wet, and temperature cycled to kickstart sugar caramelization inside each kernel before roasting even occurs. Other specialty grains impart spicy rye, grassy raw oats, earthy buckwheat, velvety oatmeal, and more when steeped briefly in the "mash" stage separate from the main mash, converting starch to fermentable sugars. Later in the boil, toast-evoking melanoidins formed by the boil infuse rich malt presence, too.

Notice comparing essential pale maltiness to bready, nutty or wi,ny notes from scaled up portions of caramel malts. Or how additions like chocolate malt, black malt, crystal rye, or toasted oats make themselves known. Taste your way along nature's incredible spectrum.

Hops Contributions

Now shift sensory gears into the wide horizons of hops - those herbaceous dried flowers of the hop vine imparting balancing bitterness along with fruity, spicy, and earthy joy. Traditional "noble hops" of central Europe – Saaz, Hallertauer, Tettnang, Spalt – tend toward spicy, floral and slightly fruity expressions of bitterness. But American hops bred over the past 50 years feature intense tropical and citrus flavors pairing beautifully with ever-growing craft palates.

Modern American hops like Amarillo, Simcoe, Mosaic, Citra and Galaxy burst with sticky, sweet orange, mango, passionfruit, pineapple and lychee impressions. Hops like Chinook and Columbus kick bitterness up a few notches. Herbal, piney, resinous greenness comes from stalwarts such as Cascade, Centennial, Willamette, and Sterling. The list of descriptor tags goes on and on for eccentric darling varieties such as Azacca, Vic Secret, Idaho 7 and experimental numbered ones too. Old school earthy English hops like Fuggle, East Kent Golding and Target also still find room to shine.

When assessing hop aromas, attune your nose and tongue to detect dense, drying bitterness aside from lighter, bright flavor notes painting their own impressionist images. Separate out grassy, herbal qualities from tropical, stone fruit or melon. Note spice expressions: is that black pepper, clove, cinnamon or dank cannabis coming through? Hops exist as a world unto themselves that enthusiastic exploration reveals little by little over time.

The Fruity Esters of Yeast

Finally we arrive at yeast, the friendly fungi feasting gleefully on sugars, churning out the magical elixirs we so enjoy. During fermentation, byproducts called esters and phenols tag along, ringing fruity or spicy bells. Hundreds of yeast strains that perform distinct flavor roles are available, either occurring naturally or cultured in labs.

As with specialty malts and trending hops, unique yeast experimentation in the craft brewing surge means flavor complexity from these microbes sees no end. However, among standard strains, certain traits mark each one. Estery English ale yeast often gives apple, pear, orange or berry hints. Belgian yeasts drive playful bubblegum, peppery phenols or banana with clove spice. Cleaner American or German lager yeasts provide a round malty or dry-hopped palate suited respectively to offer balance without interference. How do the esters or phenols blend into a cohesive experience?

Even fermentation temperature tweaks yeast metabolism toward specific aromatic paths. Excellent conditions near 50°F mute much except clean alcohol notes as in traditional pilsners, but warm ones peaking over 70°F encourage a riot of fruity ester development perfect for bold Belgian ales. Funkier strains purposefully bring earthy barnyard and rustic leather qualities, too when desired. Yeast wholly embodies one-celled creativity!

Embrace Your Personal Palate

After breaking apart basic tastes and then parsing aromatic influences from malt, hops and yeast, reassemble back into a cohesive picture naming what you detect in each sip of beer. Eventually, faced with a flight of samples, you'll be able to verbally walk through the structured process of identifying sweetness, bitterness, alcohol heat and fermentation fingerprints as second nature.

Confidence comes through practice. At first, stemware seeming overflowing with intricate impressions can overwhelm attempts to sort it all into neat descriptors. But flavor isolation gets easier with conscious repetition. Your palate is as unique as your fingerprint. Embrace what you perceive without worrying how it compares. If grapefruit bursts from a dank IPA for you while pine rules for others, who's to argue? A little wine-taster vocabulary may help, but feel free inventing your own images. Creatively paint sensory impressions in colorful phrases. Granular details emerge naturally in their own good time. For now, thoroughly enjoy taking the thoughtful journey.

Transitional Note on Critical Evaluation

Before moving on to structured tasting techniques that blend subjective preferences with more critical sensory analysis when necessary, take pleasure first in following flavor wherever it leads untethered. Unwrap fermentation characteristics layer by layer, like kids savoring Christmas gifts, too excited to care about saving fancy bows or ribbons. Chasing tastes you particularly enjoytrains the mind perhaps faster than rigid analysis sometimes anyway. So while, later we'll explore evaluating beers more objectively when the need calls for judging merit in competition or troubleshooting problems, for now simply revel in the freedom of personal discovery!

Hops, Malt, Yeast, and Water

Chapter 14

Beer and Food pairings

Beer and food can form magnificent partnerships, each bringing out new flavors and nuances in the other. Whether enjoying a simple snack alongside your homebrew or curating a tailored tasting menu, thoughtfully pairing beer and food is one of the great pleasures any brewer or food lover can experience.

This chapter will explore the art and science behind these pairings, demystifying the principles that create magic when beer meets food. We'll highlight classic combinations while also ving into experimental territories with unexpected matches that will wow your taste buds. You'll learn to predict which brews complement which foods and why by understanding key flavors, intensities, textures, and contrasts.

Our journey starts by establishing two key concepts - resonance and contrast. Resonant combinations see flavors in the beer mirrored by complementary flavors in the food. The citrusy bite of an American IPA resonates with the zesty pop of lemon chicken, just as the roasty richness found in stouts and porters resonates with smoky, charred meats or mole-laden chili. When flavors sing together in harmony across your palate, you've found resonance.

Meanwhile, contrast sees differences play off one another excitingly. The lip-puckering tartness of a fruity Berliner Weisse contrasts wildly with something sweet, such as a strawberry shortcake. The same sour beer could also contrast beautifully with salty foods like soft pretzels, brightening all the flavors. Through accentuating differences, contrast keeps our palates intrigued bite after bite.

Using resonance and contrast as guiding principles, we can approach beer and food pairings with intent instead of just guessing randomly. As we'll explore, certain beer styles and essential flavors tend to resonate or contrast better with certain styles of cuisine. Understanding these patterns in the context of intensity, texture, and overall balance on the palate clears a path for harmony and excitement.

Match Strengths Wisely

The intensity and complexity of flavors play a massive role in pairing success. Solid and aggressive beers often combine best with equally hearty foods. Consider how well smoky Russian imperial stouts resonate with a peppery pot roast laden with root vegetables. Subtler foods would get dominated and overpowered, failing to add their voice to the chorus on your palate. Lighter beers, meanwhile, suit milder dishes so their delicate notes don't vanish beneath more intense flavors. Sipping a crisp pilsner with seafood ceviche allows both to shine.

Consider the spectrum from light and delicate to strong and heavy when pairing intensity. Lean towards resonance in the middle of the spectrum and contrast at the extremes. For example, pair subtle helles lagers with equally delicate trout almondine (resonance) or ramp up the contrast with spicy buffalo wings (contrast). Weight and texture also play vital roles here. Generally, lighter beers suit lighter fare, while fuller-bodied brews match fuller textures and heavier foods.

Understanding Flavor Resonance

Now that we understand balancing intensities, let's break down the flavor resonances that define classic beer and food pairings celebrated worldwide.

For hop-forward brews like IPAs bursting with citrus, pine, tropical, and s, tone fruit flavors resonate by pairing with similarly bright, aromatic foods. Herb-roasted chicken, grilled shrimp skewers with mango salsa, peach glazed pork chops, vegetable curries lush with cilantro and lime, or even a hoppy IPA cheese ball all highlight these fruity hop flavors. The prominently malty sweetness of Scottish ales and bocks resonatesiously with caramelized flavors prominent in dishes like honey-glazed ham with raisin sauce or molasses-baked beans.

With Belgian ales, unique yeast strains' distinctive esters and phenols resonate tastefully with the warmth of spices, herbs, and ripe fruit flavors. Pair your Belgian Blonde with beet arugula salad garnished with blood orange segments and toasted walnuts. Or offer a farmhouse table dubbel alongside braised chicken thighs with figs and a dash of thyme. There is a similar resonance between clove, nutmeg, and cinnamon phenols with autumnal baked goods like pumpkin raisin muffins or apple crostatas warm from the oven.

The Roastiness of Stouts and Porters

For darker beers like stouts and porters, the essential flavors are roasted malt, dark chocolate, and coffee notes, which pair deliciously with similarly charred or smoked dishes. Dry-rubbed barbecue ribs, smoked brisket, and mole chicken wings perfectly match a robust porter, resonating with those dark beer flavors. For dessert pairings with your oatmeal or milk stout, reach for chocolate-based treats like brownies, chocolchocolate-coveredels, or the quintessential stout float with vanilla bean ice cream.

Sour and Belgian Funk

Now we venture into the tart, funky realm of sour ales and wild Belgians, which present their pairing challenges due to intense acidity. These sharp flavors resonate best with equally tart or acidic ingredients like citrus, yogurt, or vinegar. Try pairing a gueuze or Berliner Weisse with lemon arugula salad dressed lightly with olive oil and goat cheese. For a fusion twist, balance your Brett farmhouse ale with fish tacos topped with fresh lime, avocado, and red cabbage slaw. When sour fruit beers come gushing out of your homebrew pipeline, please pleasure your palate by playing with complementary fruit combinations in the glass and on the plate. A kriek lambic would sing alongside fresh cherry preserves and goat cheese crostini; raspberry sour with lemon curd tarts would create bliss.

Crisp and Clean Refreshment

Light, crisp, and delicately flavored lager styles connect naturally with herbal, grassy flavors, light meats, and shellfish. The classic example sees German-style pilsners paired brilliantly with bratwursts sizzling on the barbecue, dressed simply in mustard and sauerkraut on a pretzel bun. Staying with German tradition, a refreshing Munich Helles harmonizes taste bud heaven when sipping alongside schnitzel. For Czech pilsners, try crispy fried chicken seasoned vibrantly with paprika and parsley or seared scallops nestled on a lemony orzo. Northern English brown ales are the perfect match when fish and chips are on deck, cleansing the palate after each piping hot, malt vinegar-drizzled bite.

Beyond the Classics

While the classic pairings above connect through obvious flavor resonance, don't limit yourself solely to these combinations. Part of the splendor in pairing beer and food comes from stepping beyond these expected matches to harmonize magnificently with the unexpected. Keep the principles of resonance and contrast ever present as you freestyle with flavors, textures, and styles on the glass and the plate.

For curiously adventurous palates, dabble in unusual yet delightful pairings that still follow the core maxim of matching intensities. How about a rich, velvety imperial stout alongside luxurious seared foie gras? Or provide a shocking contrast to ultra-hoppy double IPAs with mild, smooth burrata sprinkled with sea salt and olive oil. Belgian dubbels bring dried fruit esters and spicy phenols to marry beautifully with mole poblano layered with bittersweet Mexican chocolate. Take a traditional gose brewed with coriander and salt to new heights paired with salted caramel gelato. The possibilities for harmony – or intentional contrast - indeed run boundless for those bold enough to deviate from norms.

Certain flavors tend to complement practically anything served alongside. Herbal, rustic saisons offer versatility to match light salads, hearty roasts, and everything between with their delicate earthy spice and lemon-citrus brightness. Chocolatey yet roasty brown ales also pair delightfully with nearly all barbecue and Tex-Mex dishes, sweet bakery treats, and other flavorful foods. Only restrict yourself to classics after testing these broadly food-friendly beers to accompany unlikely table fellows.

When Intensity Collides

Now for a crucially important warning regarding intensity mismatches: Avoid radical clashes where very bold, aggressive beers meet delicately flavored cuisine. Disasters often unfold when an über-hoppy West Coast imperial IPA arrives uninvited to a garden salad party, dominating meek greens instead of integrating harmoniously. Similarly, subtle golden lagers drowned beneath intensely hot Buffalo wings or bitter chocolate desserts, unfortunately mute the nuance each delicacy offers.

Study the flavors and intensity before committing to pair drastically different foods and beers, or experiments may transpose poorly to the palate. A significantly more potent brew demands an equally intense plate mate, while gentler beers request dishes of comparable delicacy to duet successfully. Trust resonance and contrast to guide, aligning potency appropriately on both sides of the glass and plate.

The Art of Pairing Brews with Bites

Having explored key successful combinations alongside missteps to avoid, let's summarize tips for thoughtfully pairing your beers with bites every brew session.

Start by considering intensity upfront, determining if the flavors at hand suggest a resonant pairing or intentional contrast makes sense. Treat truly delicate beers and dishes as you would fine glassware – with care to find complementary elements so neither shatters nor overshadows. For heartier builds on both sides, decide whether resonance through doubling down on shared robust flavors or providing contrast makes the most sense tastebud-wise.

From here, determine where specific flavors of your beer and potential plates fall across the critical dimensions outlined earlier. Which characteristics outshine intensely: Herbal hops? Roasted malt? Fruit esters? Chocolate? These prominent notes in a break offer compass points towards cuisine with similar or deliberately contrasting earmarks. If flavors feel random or unclear in the beer or dish, simpler is generally safer. Clean, crisp pilsners or Helles harmonize broadly rather than competing chaotically across the palate.

The dining table offers endless opportunities for delightful discovery through pairing brews with bites. Hopefully, these guiding principles equip you to curate perfect beer flights for every course and craving confidently! Trust in resonance, respect contrast judiciously, align intensities, and above all - follow both heart and head by simply enjoying two of life's greatest gifts: good beer and great food in joyful harmony. Cheers!

Chapter 15

Experimenting with fruit, spice, and other flavor additions

While traditional beer ingredients create endless recipe options, exploring flavor additions user us into a new world of creative possibilities! The slightest dash of spice, squeeze of citrus, or spoonful of jam can dramatically enhance and expand beer profiles when done thoughtfully. Just a pinch takes clean beers to new heights; too heavy a hand overpowers entirely.

This chapter explores ingredients that infuse haunting aromas, lively flavors, and vivid colors when integrated skillfully into brew sessions or fermentation. We'll cover choosing quality fruits, spices, and other flavorings for maximum impact – without disruption or dangerous compounds. While fruits and botanicals inspire many ideas here due to their natural synergy, don't limit yourself only to these categories when dreaming up flavor combinations!

Fruity Inspirations

From tropical mangoes or tart cherries to juicy boysenberries or gentle elderflowers, fruits of all forms inject vivid personality into beers when appropriately handled. Brewers build entire brands around masterfully fruited sours, with legendary raspberry or apricot lambics setting the standard. Fruits introduce tartness, tannins, sweetness, herbal complexity, and unmistakable aromas during fermentation or secondary conditioning, depending on the method and desired intensity.

Not all fruits play nicely in beer, though, due to fickle fermentability, tricky pH levels, or extracting vegetal flavors. Sturdy stone fruits and hardy berries usually fare best, while melons and delicate berries often disappoint without extra finesse. Underripe fruit brings harsh, sour greenness, like overripe fruit turns cloyingly sweet and rotten instead of plump and juicy. Mind fruit quality, fermentability potential, and ideal beer styles carefully when conceptualizing your flavor fusion vision.

When fruit shines at peak ripeness with balanced sweet-tart depth, wonderful alchemy unfolds! Raspberries, blackberries, sour cherries, peaches, and apricots ferment beautifully into stunning lambics and tart Flanders reds. Thanks to complementary hop aromas already in the mix, Citrus zest electrifies American and Belgian ales.

Even starchy bananas and plantains lend surprisingly luscious bodies and flavors when caramelized into South Asian spiced ales or tart and roasty Inca Chicha de Jora corn beers. Pit fruits like plums and peaches pair easily with malty English bitters by contributing delicate stone fruit essence. And virtually all fruits harmonize with bready hefeweizens by doubling on banana goodness!

When using any fruit, introduce either during secondary fermentation once primary yeast activity ceases or directly in the serving keg/cask to avoid disrupting delicate fermentation. Pasteurizing purées prevents pathogenic intrusions without losing personality. Know your base beer style well before just tossing fruit puree into primary fermentation – what complements traditional clove phenols of German weizens contrasts IPAs bursting with New World hops.

Botanical Infusions

Herbs and flowers also channel magical aromas and flavors when skillfully aligned with underlying beer foundations. Noble European hops first provided the herbal spice that defines beer itself. Garden-fresh rosemary, sage, basil, thyme, and oregano build upon herbal hop vibes in modern renditions of ancient gruit ales. Gentle lavender, jasmine, and honeysuckle blooms conduct graceful floral aromas into fruited sours or farmhouse saisons without overpowering them.

Resinous bay leaf, earthy wormwood, vibrant lemon verbena - your farmer's market offers inspiration at every turn! For guidance, look towards regional food specialties featuring herbs and botanicals paired deliciously with local beers over generations. Belgium's straightforward golden ales traditionally contain a graceful hint of orange peel supporting fruity fermentation character – easy inspiration for beginner brewers to grasp. Bolder red ales from the same region feature hints of anise complimenting caramel malt backbones.

In the herb-obsessed Middle East, mint makes refreshing company for Egyptian soured barley beers while potent za'atar spice blends Egyptian Stingo beers brilliantly. Cardamom pods infuse aromatically smooth Kvarken Cloudberry Ale flavored with foraged golden berries. While choosing herbs, remember that a little goes a long way before unbridled vegetation negates malt and hop balance! Start conservatively with any unknown herb mix and increase gently in future batches if the desired signature remains elusive.

Once fruit or herbs beckon alluringly, we must select compatible styles to build upon. European ales frequently provide inviting starting points thanks to delicate malt foundations, allowing botanical flavors to stage for elaborate expression. Hop-forward American styles often overshadow subtler plant notes unless fused intentionally as a contrast. Attempting to highlight soft rose hips within a profoundly piney West Coast IPA usually ends poorly!

Spice Blends Across Cultures

Building upon herbs and botanicals, let's explore the countless global spices that bring magical new dimensions to beer. European classics frequently highlight spices lining medieval pantry shelves – cinnamon, nutmeg, allspice berries, and cloves for warming winter ales. Belgians utilize orange peel and coriander in many lighter brews; in darker dubbels and tripels, aniseed and cumin make cameos.

These provide perfect starting points for freestyling new spice blends to accent malt bills. Complementary but safe options like vanilla beans, cacao nibs, Lapsang souchong tea, and chilies make easy inaugural additions even for novice brewers. Later, weave in bolder flavors like peppercorns, fenugreek, cardamom,, and licorice root once you are you are comfortable brewing balanced beers without disruption.

Some spices challenge fermentation microbiology when overdone, so no limitations. For example, Team Clostridium's nefarious members despise hop bitterness and cause serious illnesses, which are offset only by high gravities and strictly controlled fermentation. Small chili additions are delicious, but high capsaicin levels seriously hinder total alcohol production by restricting yeast growth unless appropriately addressed beforehand. Moral of the story: Follow spice addition guidelines carefully,, and never toss handfuls of unknowns into a batch without guidance!

If venturing into ethnic spice realms beyond European origins, respect styles that evolved across intricate culinary cultures over generations. Learn traditional usage rates and combinations for items like Chinese five-spice powder or Indian garam masala seasoning blends before Americanizing eitherumpkin ale experiments without context. Some epic wins emerge through intentionally fusing disparate traditions, but also spectacular failures!

Understanding the balance of complex aromatic essential oils of ginger, sandalwood, turmeric, and fenugreek from Indian cuisine requires practice so as not to overwhelm delicate malts. Similarly,, hop-forward American interpretations of traditional Mexican mole beers flop regularly by suffocating distinctive chili-chocolate-cinnamon interplay. In these cases,, we must dial exotic back, not race forward haphazardly.

When deviating into the unknown, keemeticulousus notes on tweaked recipes and fermentation behaviors with unfamiliar variables in play to learn for the next rounds. Maybe ysiphonedbon-soaked oak chips siphoned glorious vanilla earthiness as planned into the chocolate oatmeal stout...or perhaps too much tannin seeped instead from sloppy wood prep, requiring refinement before our barrel-aged dream emerged appropriately. Detailed brew journals prevent painful repeats of costly mistakes!

Infusing Food Elements

Thus far, we have focused on fruits, herbs, and straight spices as additions that trigger magical metamorphoses in our brewing crucibles. However, don't limit yourself solely to plain-Jane ingredients in raw natural forms! Also, consider infusing finished beers during conditioning with spice mixes, butter, roasted flavors, sweeteners, and other derivative food elements that incorporate fantastic flavors.

A pat of ginger cardamom compound butter stirred gently into the secondary can impart incredible aromatic complexity superior to raw spices tossed carelessly. Infusing small batches with multiple tea bag types like chamomile vanilla or Moroccan mint unveils subtle sophistication through herbal tannins. Stirring a spoonful of bourbon barrel-aged maple syrup into the keg before carbonation allows wood and vanilla to shine brighter than over-making with spirals during fermentation.

The range of possibilities through food derivatives and flavor infusions climbs exponentially once we detach from plain fruits or lone spices! Consider orange chocolate mole stout aged gens on a chocolate-dipped oak spiral for a flavor rollercoaster engulfing the palate. Or tart berry lambic conditioned briefly on bags of mixed berry tea and lemon zest before serving.

Ensure infusing adjuncts during secondary fermentation or conditioning instead of primary avoids skewing delicate microbiological balance. Yeast can only handle so much complexity at once before quality slips. Also, embrace prudence with residual sugars or added alcohol from flavoring agents by allowing a little extra conditioning time for the yeast to calibrate correctly before packaging. Rushing beer with a heavy hand into bottles or kegs risks over carbonation or even exploding bottles from reactivated fermentation!

While suggestions here provide ample inspiration for initial forays, never feel restricted only to known ingredients in familiar forms. Those feeling especially adventurous can even take beer flavor additions in avant-garde directions far beyond the fruits, spices, and derivatives described above. How about infusing coconut, almonds, and turmeric into a sweet stout inspired by exotic kheer rice pudding? Or maybe green tea and bergamot siphoned from loose-leaf Earl Grey tea bags to transform a high-ABV tripel into an aromatic black tea-infused sipper?

Fantastic flavors await explorers traveling far off the beaten path – just remember to keep one foot firmly planted by taking prudent process precautions as you reach the unknown! With openness balanced by sound technical understanding, creativity gushes boundlessly when experimenting with additions. Just maintain detailed logs since not every novel idea transfers easily from the imagination onto our palates. But with careful tweaking and repetition, spectacular originality inevitably emerges through joining pioneering brewers pushing boundaries ever further into uncharted territory. So toss conservatism aside – and adventure on!

Hops, Malt, Yeast, and Water

Chapter 16

Gifting and Serving Homebrew

Nothing satisfies more than sharing the fruits of your labor with appreciative audiences after brewing batches of glorious homebrew in your cobbled-together garage nano-brewery. Whether gifting bottles to friends and family or hosting formal tastings after much testing and refinement, understand first impressions matter greatly when others first savor your beer.

This closing chapter offers tips on adequately presenting homebrew for maximum enjoyment in casual or formal settings. First, we'll cover ideal methods for packaging and transporting bottles or kegs to avoid messy disasters en route to the event. Proper glassware, pouring technique, food pairings, and tasting sheets also factor in when serving, so we'll detail best practices to impress guests.

Finally, guidance on writing tasteful accompanying cards or signage adds personalized touches, elevating your brand reputation through classy detailing. Follow these tips whenever sharing your beers – regardless of whether it is a small backyard cookout, wedding reception, or fully immersive twelve-course beer dinner paired spectacularly from first pour to final nightcap.

Careful Transport and Serving Logistics

Getting beer safely to any event without leakage or breakage takes thought, particularly when traveling distances or juggling multiple fragile bottles and unwieldy kegs. Thankfully, several products exist to ease transport stress for personal brewers.

First, procure milk crates, six-pack holders, or sturdy cardboard boxes specifically sized for secure beer transport. These keep individually capped bottles separated and cushioned when stacking layers prevent josprevent route. Fill gaps with packing material to inhibit crashing bottle collisions. Harsher bumps cause foamy messes once caps release, so indulge your cargo! Consider bubble wrap or air pocket packing materials around bottles before boxing up.

For lifting hefty kegs using modified refrigerators as "jockey boxes," attach conveniently wheeled dolly platforms, allowing easy single-person transport over uneven terrain into venues. Dispensing lines stay protected by rolling inside until safely connected to tap faucets only when securely in place at your destination. Backup cylinders of CO2 gas fuel the system once taps start flowing, so kegs pour perfectly chilled beer on demand without relying on external refrigeration onsite.

When possible, utilize portable folding tables to serve as makeshift bars for an organization rather than scatter bottles randomly across existing counters and tables. Tablecloths add class while corralling spills, and empties are easily cleaned afterward. Arrange glassware, bottle openers, tasting sheets, and other accessories needed before guests arrive, so pouring commences quickly at service time. Nobody likes standing around thirstily awaiting beer. They glimpsed and lugged past en route inside because the brewer fumbled, finding essential serving tools! Plan.

Presenting with Style

Beyond safely getting beer to the venue, half the enjoyment stems from on-point presentation, elevating perceived quality when initially served. Start by stocking properly sized glassware for each style you'll pour. Sturdy pint glasses work okay for casual situations, although pilsners, weizen vases, snifters, and tulip glasses better accentuate aromatics for their respective beer styles when possible. Craft beer demands respect through tailored vessels, so supply variety - don't force your English bitter into ketchup-stained Shrek souvenir mugs!

Nothing screams novice like recklessly pouring straight down the middle of the glass, creating aggressive foaming everywhere except inside the actual glass. The tilt is appropriately angled around 45 degrees until half full, then eased back vertically, allowing the controlled foam to surface attractively. Leave ample headspace at the top for nose-tickling aromatics to gather instead of spilling over the rim wastefully because you misjudged distances as the tap faucet recedes upwards.

If bottling, incorporate nicely branded custom caps or peel-off labels denoting beer names rather than expecting guests to guess contents randomly. However, avoid tacky neon fonts or clashing colors detracting from the classic beer elegance people anticipate once poured. Fashion simple tying tags for bottlenecks denoting brew specifics like commercial Belgian ales do for easy identification when served amongst multiple homebrew options.

Extra Touches

Additional touches enhance enjoyment by providing valuable details, delicious pairings, and aesthetically pleasing visual components beyond flawless pours alone.

Designing tasting sheets preprinted with your beer names allows guests space to record live reactions, scaling intensity of perceived hoppiness, maltiness, bitterness, and overall impressions sip by sip as they experience multiple brew options. Structured evaluation forms prevent forgetting opinions that inform your rebrewing decisions later.

Pair essential foods that accommodate a wide range of beer styles instead of intensive dishes matching specific offerings. Pretzels, nuts, crackers, and mild cheeses pair deliciously with most beers, so emphasize unanimous crowd-pleasers over divisive plates unless your menu intentionally harmonizes multiple courses with advanced beer pairings, dish by dish.

Finally, incorporate appropriate decorative touches respecting the brewing craft without crossing into kitschy themes unrelated to the beer. Classy tap handles engraved with your home brewery logo, hop wreaths across the bar, live edge wood signage illuminating names - all perfectly acceptable. But also, only pumpkins and hay bales are oddly positioned if intentionally pouring harvest seasonals! Keep supplemental decor classy and aligned with artisanal beer to maintain on-brand cohesion across the entire tasting experience.

Written Words of Wisdom

With transport, presentation, and pairings perfected, focus on attached branding conveying style names, tasting notes, and personalized messages from the brewmaster in writing. Elevate beyond cheap computer paper printouts by using heavier cardstock matching the color scheme of your homemade beer labels for an upscale look.

Create a consistent format including style name, ABV, IBUs, ideal serving temperature, tasting notes, and food pairings with each printed or written recipe. Stylistic choices abound here - accented calligraphy with quill pens adds artistic panache to scrolls. Or emulate antique bounty flyers from the Old West with faux parchment and dripping inks describing rewards for locating your brews across dusty saloon bars!

Craft thoughtful greeting cards for each recipient when gifting bottles, mentioning the specific beer style inside and why you selected them to sample that recipe. Add a personal message like, "Thought of our college days savoring Belgian sours at Brew Ha Ha in Providence...I hope my raspberry lambic sour transports us right back to those late nights once you pry off that cork! Salut - Ethan"

Even minimalism communicates elegance and confidence, letting pristinely labeled bottles speak volumes without supplementary frills. Ultimately, you determine the pairing personality between beer liquid and written branding.

Ensure consistency across all packaging elements, wall signage, and drinkware to reinforce the sophisticated visual impact. Consumers immersed in that cohesive experience perceive heightened quality emanating throughout.

Now filled with ideas on safely transporting, properly presenting, and thoughtfully branding your homebrewed creations, the stage is set to deliver unforgettable moments when you crack open these beers for old and new friends. Confidence as a gracious host pours forth flawlessly once preparation culminates in serving your spectacular ales exactly how they deserve. So get brewing, and here's to many happy returns where your beers gather loved ones together in merry appreciation of your edible crafting talents from now until the last call! Cheers to that.